10-19-09

To Ed & Brenda Power,
Our Long Time Friends.
Hope You enjoy The True Romance
Adventure-Love Stories of a
Young Sailor.

Wally WWII

"RIVER OF LOVE"
BY WAY OF
A WAR

True Stories by:
Wally Hillman

U.S. Navy – 1943 – 1947
Atlantic Fleet
"Tin Can Sailor"

Copyright © 2008 by Wally Hillman

All rights reserved. No part of this book shall be reproduced or transmitted in any form or by any means, electronic, mechanical, magnetic, photographic including photocopying, recording or by any information storage and retrieval system, without prior written permission of the publisher. No patent liability is assumed with respect to the use of the information contained herein. Although every precaution has been taken in the preparation of this book, the publisher and author assume no responsibility for errors or omissions. Neither is any liability assumed for damages resulting from the use of the information contained herein.

ISBN 0-7414-4765-7

Published by:

1094 New DeHaven Street, Suite 100
West Conshohocken, PA 19428-2713
Info@buybooksontheweb.com
www.buybooksontheweb.com
Toll-free (877) BUY BOOK
Local Phone (610) 941-9999
Fax (610) 941-9959

Printed in the United States of America

Printed on Recycled Paper

Published February 2009

In Tribute

Especially to those young men I trained with in Boot Camp, Bainbridge, MD, January 1944, Company 3001. I know that many of you left your family behind and volunteered, just as I did, at seventeen years of age, to defend our homeland against those who dare threaten our loved ones and challenge our way of life.

To those of you who went directly to the Pacific fleet where the greatest sea battles ever recorded in history, before or since, occurred. Many of you did not return to your families, some did not make it to your eighteenth birthday. I salute you and pay the highest tribute one shipmate can pay to another. You made the ultimate sacrifice.

Wally Hillman

"There are no flowers on a sailor's grave."

(German Sailor's song)

Preface

These writings are not about WWII. Although the war was the vehicle that brought us together at just the right moment for both of us. Katherine was not in a serious relationship with anyone and neither was I. She had been in Norfolk about one year when I first saw her. Of course she had dated during that time; she was a stunning, beautiful, young woman with just enough freckles to betray her farm girl, exposed to the sun upbringing. She exuded a disarming aura of no pretend, Southern Belle, shy, genteel innocence. She tended to avoid eye contact when guys and even women looked admiringly at her. I consider the absolute pinnacle of my physical life was the first moment I saw my Katherine. There was no "Guardian Angel" this time. It was as though God himself said to me right then, "There she is, the one I have prepared just for you since before you were born. Now let's see if you have what it takes to win her love."

I had no long-term plans, the only thing important to me was looking forward to reenlisting in the Navy and the "round the world cruise" my ship was scheduled to start in a few months. Suddenly, those things were no longer important to me. Thoughts and visions of this lady were on my mind.

True to her Christian heritage, she has been a loving, faithful, devoted, wonderful wife and mother, and I know, someday, one of God's chosen angels.

Introduction

The following is a list of remarkable similarities between Katherine and me and our families.

1. The River joined our lives together since we were born.

    About <u>15</u> <u>miles</u> from my home in Roanoke, VA, two rivers, The North Fork and The South Fork, come together forming the head waters and <u>beginning</u> of the <u>Roanoke River</u>, "The River of Love", which meanders southeasterly for three hundred eighty miles, ending near the North Carolina Town of Plymouth. On an active, working tobacco farm about <u>15</u> <u>miles</u> from the <u>end</u> of the <u>Roanoke River</u>, near Pinetown, on Long Ridge Road, lived a lovely seventeen year old farm girl named:

    Katherine <u>Elizabeth</u> <u>Jackson</u>

2. My mother's first name is <u>Elizabeth</u>

3. My father's middle name is <u>Jackson</u>

4. Each of our last names has <u>seven</u> <u>letters</u> and each ends with an <u>"N"</u>

5. The last three letters of our last names are <u>man</u> and <u>son</u>

6. Katherine's mother was <u>older</u> than her father

7. Katherine is <u>older</u> than me

8. Katherine's father's birthday is in the month of <u>December</u>
9. Katherine's mother's birthday is August <u>22</u>nd
10. My birthday is <u>December</u> 22nd
11. Each of our mothers had a male baby that died shortly after birth
12. Each of our mothers had five boys before having a girl baby.
13. Katherine and I were each a middle child.
14. We each had <u>two</u> brothers born between us and our baby sister.
15. I was a crewman aboard the Navy Destroyer USS <u>Harold</u> <u>James</u> Ellison.
16. Katherine had two older brothers named <u>Harold</u> and <u>James</u>
17. We both had identical color blonde hair.

Last but not least,

18. The distance from my home to her home was the exact same distance as her home was to my home. Yuk, yuk, yuk

"RIVER OF LOVE"

December 7, 1941, the odyssey begins. The next six years would bring adventures I could never have dreamed of, far away places, different cultures – people – ways of life, some friendly, some not. Extreme dangers, excitement, disappointments, fears, tears, deaths, surprises, many challenges, and accomplishments. Later, love – jealousy – deceit – misunderstandings – phone calls – lies – bragging – macho tales. But in the end, the reward was love and happiness for life.

* * * * *

I was born and raised in the growing railroad town of Roanoke, Virginia at the southern end of the great Shenandoah Valley, nestled in a quiet, serene, beautiful valley on the banks of the Roanoke River, my "River of Love," surrounded by the majestic Blue Ridge Mountains to the east and south, the Appalachian Mountains to the west. I had spent the first fifteen years of my life in Roanoke, venturing out, at the most, a few hundred miles. Now that was about to change.

* * * * *

Having lived though the great depression years, like everyone else, I had jobs to do whether I was paid or not. My paying job was selling and delivering the local newspaper. I paid three cents for the papers and sold them for five cents.

Sunday, December 7, my papers were all delivered by 8:00 AM, leaving time to get ready with my family to go to church and Sunday school which started at 9:00 AM. We returned home about 12:30 to a great dinner prepared by my mom, yes, I said dinner; lunch was food we put in a bag. The next meal was supper. Going to church Sunday morning was something everyone did in those days. I cannot remember even one family that did not attend the church of their choice.

Sunday, 12:30 – December 7, 1941 – Eastern Time, the cowardly attack at Pearl Harbor by the Japanese was well under way.

My family of five boys and one baby sister were whiling away the hours doing whatever we normally did on a quiet, winter Sunday afternoon. About 5:00 PM we began noticing people coming out of their homes, gathering in small groups, and talking in hushed tones among themselves. Gradually, the groups began coming together, their words growing louder with angry and frightening tones as more news came in about a place called Pearl Harbor, which no one had ever heard of. News traveled slowly then, no television, no computers, no satellites.

Unknown to us, during those few hours, our lives, and the lives of every person on earth, and those to come were forever changed. Millions were destined to die during the next five years.

December 7, 1941, our newspaper printed a special, late, "Extra Edition" with large black five inch, bold headlines announcing: "Japanese Attack Pearl Harbor". At this time President Roosevelt had not declared war on the Empire of Japan.

All newspaper boys were out late into the night, selling door to door, the special Extra Edition for five cents each. I sold hundreds. Now, I would pay hundreds of dollars for one of the original papers I sold for a nickel.

The stage was now set for my meeting Katherine, the love of my life, six years later.

December 7, 1941, Katherine was seventeen years old. Like all farm girls, she had many jobs to do. This was early Sunday morning and she was busy helping her mother prepare breakfast for a family of ten on a wood burning cook stove. They used wood from their own stand of trees, eggs laid that morning by hens that were hatched from last year's flock, bacon from hogs grown on the farm, beef, fresh milk, and butter from their cows, other meats from game hunted or trapped in surrounding forests, honey from their own bee hives, jelly and jams from apple, pear, and peach trees, grapes from their grape vines, strawberries picked from the patch, wild berries from the woods, and corn bread and dumplings from the corn field. Every kind of vegetable, fresh or canned, grown right on the farm along with large, sweet watermelons in the good ole summertime. The only foods they had to buy with money earned from their farm crops were staples like sugar and flour by the barrel. Even today, grandchildren speak fondly and with watering mouths about the biscuits grandma Jackson whipped up in the pantry just off the kitchen, using a large wooden mixing bowl that grandpa hand carved out of cypress from a nearby swamp. After breakfast the entire family attended church as they had most every Sunday all their lives. When they were younger, the family piled onto a two wheeled, mule drawn cart for the five mile trip, each way, to church. If it was cold they bundled up close to each other, in winter coats and plenty of handmade blankets.

Unknown to the family, in a place on earth more than four thousand miles away they had never heard of, Pearl Harbor, events were unfolding at that very moment that forever would change each of their lives. It was the first turn of the wheel, the first step on the path that would lead Katherine to the man who would become the father of her children. Their church was located in the small farming community town of Pinetown, NC. Five miles of unpaved, sandy, Long Ridge road to the church their father helped build, winding through tobacco, corn and soybean fields. Five miles back to the one-fourth mile lane leading to the large, white farm house, lay the well kept, eighty-nine acre Jackson farm. There were no utilities, electric, phone, or water coming to the house or any other in the area. Katherine is the first daughter, born into a hard working, well liked, respected, God fearing, church going family of nine children. Her father and mother were two of the last genuine, old time pioneers. He was a jack-of-all-trades type of man, building houses, barns, farming, barber, community doctor, etc. She was a strong, faithful, hard working, devoted wife and mother who bore him nine children, all in the same room of the house that he built, adding rooms as his family grew larger. He was known for his delicious country hams. When each of his nine babies was born, the doctor asked for and received one of his hams, hand cured as only he knew his special way. When they were married he had a job in Pinetown working for the railroad. He inherited eighty-nine acres of swamp and woodland from his father. They cut timber, dug hundreds of tree stumps, cleared thick, briar filled, poisonous snake infested underbrush, dug canals to drain the swamp, and dug wells for fresh water. They went into this hostile environment and carved out a working, producing farm, almost totally self sustaining, that provided for their family and a wonderful place to raise children for generations to come. I really regret not having the chance to meet and talk with John Jackson. I have great admiration for a man like this and the wonderful woman who supported him, a wife and mother God made just for a man like him. I can see a lot of her in my Katherine. They had a battery powered radio which was used sparingly to hear weather reports and farm news. Bad news has a way of spreading and soon they knew something very bad had happened, but like all Americans, did not realize how much it would affect each of them.

Katherine's high school sweetheart was a popular young man; they were both the same age. He was musically talented, played the guitar, and sang with a group on the radio, small clubs in the area, and the choir at the Baptist church. Her dad was the typical dad of the time, she was not allowed to date until she was sixteen, and then only when other girls and their dates were along, no dancing. Since there were no telephones or even electric lines in the area, plans had to be made at school about meeting in Washington, NC, on Saturday night, a twenty mile trip for her with one of her brothers. She would meet with other girls and go shopping or boyfriends to a movie. If her sweetheart was not in town he would get mad at her for going with someone else. This happened fairly often according to her little diary that she let me read.

      Katherine was a pretty, honey blonde, the tallest girl in her class, and very self conscious. She had no problem attracting the local boys. She did have a rival, another pretty blonde who liked the same boy she did. They both rode the same school bus. When the other girl got on the bus she would loudly brag about being with him the night before. Katherine fumed, but the next time she saw him she told him in no uncertain terms, "If he dated the other girl again not to ever come back to see her." This worked. When he was inducted into the army and was being sent overseas he asked her to marry him. She wisely said no but she would wait for him. She was a very sensible young woman; he was killed in November 1944 at the age of twenty during the invasion of Europe. Katherine's dad had objected to her going with him because his dad was a long time alcoholic, and he tended to go to the bottle when he became upset. She says she would probably have married him.

Her dad died May 16, 1943. She attended high school in Bath, North Carolina, "Blackbeard the Pirate's" territory. She started school in a one room schoolhouse at the end of the lane from her home on Long Ridge Road. The two teachers lived in the Jackson home. She was the first of her family, in June 1944, to graduate from high school. When she was in the sixth grade, she contracted a very contagious, at that time, disease, Scarlett Fever. The entire family was quarantined for about three months. A warning sign was posted on the house. No one could enter or leave the property during that time. Her younger sister also became sick. This caused all of the Jackson children to repeat the grade they were in.

* * * * *

December 22, 1941, I celebrated my fifteenth birthday. Early in 1942 I started working for the "Postal Telegraph", competitor of the "Western Union", the two fastest ways of delivering printed messages at the time. We messenger boys delivered envelope enclosed Morse code messages translated by typewriter all over the Roanoke Valley in rain, snow, and ice, every kind of weather on straight chain, leg powered bikes, no gears, no motors. When we left the office we had to press a time clock out and in, showing how much time we took to make deliveries, no stopping or goofing around. We knew all the shortcuts and tipping in those days was something men did with their hats. Day messengers were paid thirty cents an hour, night boys were paid thirty-five cents. I was a night messenger.

The folks in the office forgot to tell me the meaning of the star on the outside of the envelope. I learned the hard way when I delivered the first one, it meant a son or husband had been killed or was missing in action. Imagine, Christmas night, delivering a starred envelope to the home of a seventeen or eighteen year old boy who only a few years before had been waiting for Santa at that very same home. Although all the messenger boys were white, there were no sections in the city at that time where we were afraid to go. Many times at night I went down dark back alleys to find back steps to deliver a star telegram to a black family. I had the same dread because a black mother and family had the same reaction of shock and grief as a white mother and family. There were many envelope stars during that time. "The war raged on", when a single ship was torpedoed it could mean three hundred or three thousand plus lost at one time. I do not remember ever delivering a star telegram about a service woman being killed or wounded in action. Bill Clinton or N.O.W. had not been invented. The ladies did a great job taking care of the home front.

* * * * *

Just about all of my friends only one year or so older than me, were scattered all over the world in the various military services. All males eighteen and older were being drafted. The only choice we had was volunteering for the service we liked best before being drafted. Lines at all recruiting stations were filled with young men, nervous, angry, but anxious to be trained to defend their country, not the cowards of today, running away to Canada. All the while, they knew that some would die. In fact, hundreds of thousands did not return alive. Many thousands did return but not to a normal life because of injuries, physical or psychological. Many of those who could not pass the entry physical and were rejected felt disappointed, ashamed, embarrassed, and angry but went on to do their part by working in industry manufacturing war materials. Conscientious objectors volunteered as battlefield medics, etc., others went to the extreme. While on a short leave from the Navy, I learned one of my friends could not pass the physical and was turned down by the Navy. The term for this was being 4-F, unfit for military service. He was later found hanging by his neck in a tree by a little creek on a farm area where we used to play; my younger brother Chuck was one of the first on the scene. October of 1942, I learned that several of my friends had quit school and gone to Newport News, Virginia to work in the shipyards. Since my choice of military had always been the Navy, this was my chance to learn firsthand knowledge of naval fighting ships. I applied for a job and was accepted even though I was only fifteen. I fudged on my age by two months, but they desperately needed workers and did not question it. Little did I realize how much and how my life was about to change, but I was excited.

* * * * *

The distance from Roanoke to Newport News today is about five hours by interstate highways which did not exist at that time. I packed my suitcase for my first time traveling by myself. Since I had very little money, mom packed a bag full of sandwiches and apples for me to eat along the way; soft drinks were only five cents. I settled in for the three hundred fifty mile, fifteen hour bus trip through every little town, stopping to pick up or let off passengers all along the way. There were no onboard toilets, you just hoped to make it to the next town that had a bus station. Cars were not being made and gas was rationed, so most people traveled by bus or train. We traveled mostly at night and I was able to sleep as best I could. The bus was soon filled with people standing in the isle; most were for short trips. I soon learned I was lucky to have my own seat because the trip originated in Roanoke. Days before my trip, it was arranged with a family we knew, who had moved from Roanoke to Newport News, to meet me at the bus station and I was to stay with them until I could find a place of my own. The bus was darkened, after so many hours of riding, I went to sleep. I was soon to learn something that, in those days, was not discussed in proper society, at least not to children. I learned that young boys attracted a certain type of men. (This was written in 2005, I do not care what the rules are now, my description stands.)

About an hour from Newport News, I was awakened by someone standing in the isle with his arm across the back of my seat, his hand on my face rubbing my lips. I pulled away from him and he removed his arm. I went back to sleep, a short time later he did this again, only this time the man sitting next to me saw him and tried to grab his arm. He quickly moved further to the back of the bus. I was no longer sleepy; I began talking to the man sitting next to me. He was about twenty-five or thirty years old. He had worked in the ship yards for several years and began telling me about the work.

We pulled into the Newport News bus station about 5:00 AM. The friends who were to meet me were not there; I sat down and waited. Later I learned the arrival time was misunderstood, 5:00 PM not 5:00 AM. My new friend noticed I had a problem. He told me he and his wife had an apartment nearby and I could use the spare bedroom, sleep late, and he would take me to the employment office. By this time it was about an hour later and no one had come for me, we walked to his apartment. I was very tired, got in bed and fell fast asleep. Sometime later I was awakened by someone getting into bed with me, it was my new friend. I learned what this type of men do to young boys. We awoke hours later; he bought my breakfast and took me to the shipyard employment office. I was there most of the day and was to report for work at seven the next morning. I had no choice but to return to the apartment because my bag and clothes were there. He said he would talk to his wife about me renting the spare bedroom. He knew his wife would again be out of town the weekend. He wanted me to stay and meet friends he had coming over for a party. I realized later he was hoping to bring me into the homosexual lifestyle. Gay was a happy word then. They cannot create, they can only recruit.

He worked the night shift, 11:00 PM through 7:00 AM. When I arrived, his wife was back and explained she had been visiting her parents in Williamsburg. She said I was welcome to the bedroom until I found another place to stay and she also goes to work at the shipyard at 7:00 AM. I went to bed early, and later, a squeaky door woke me up; my door would not close completely and I had to go to the bathroom. I looked through the crack and saw a man go into her bedroom, it was not her husband.

* * * * *

The shipyard was a very large place; I never saw either of them again. During my first workday I was told of a rooming house one block from my gate to the shipyard. The owner of the large, three story frame house was a friendly, older Jewish lady, Mrs. Malnick. She invited me into her clean, neat living room and asked questions about my home, family, etc. I am sure she noticed I was a scared, shy kid away from home for the first time. She said she was looking for someone like me to have a small sun porch type room at the rear of her living quarters. The rent was four dollars a week and most of my meals were at a boarding house next door. They packed lunches for us each day. I am sure this was one of many times my "Guardian Angel" was taking care of me. Mrs. Malnick just took me under her wing, becoming like a second mother. Looking back from this time of my life I can see that someone surely was often watching over me. "The war raged on." I quickly settled into a daily routine: up at 6:00 AM, breakfast next door, picked up my packed "surprise" bag lunch, grabbed my newly issued hard hat and rushed one block down the street to the closest gate into the shipyard to my assigned lane through an employee check-in building.

On a wall were hundreds of quarter sized copper discs, each with an imprinted number. As each worker passed through, they called out their number and the disc was turned over so the time keepers could record who did not report for work. Again, my "Guardian Angel" was there. I had been assigned to the hull engineering department, exactly where I wanted to be, working directly on board the aircraft carriers. My job had nothing to do with the ship's hull or engineering but was a part of that department. I started as an apprentice helper with five men who did a specific job below the hanger deck throughout the ship. To lessen the possibility of sabotage, only the supervisors knew the exact end performance of the work we did. We installed control panels with pressure gauges, copper tubing that ran to panels in other parts of the ship. Aircraft carriers are literally floating cities, with a honeycomb complex of hundreds of different compartments. It would be like walking through a cave with dozens of tunnels branching off. Each compartment, each passageway, deck, and platform from bow to stern, identified with letters and numbers. Using a locator map, I was learning the inner workings of the Navy's largest fighting ships. With each control panel installed, six one inch holes had to be drilled though steel deck plates below, one small test hole was drilled and a welding rod stuck through. One of my jobs was to locate the compartment below and find the welding rod, sometimes hidden in clusters of electrical cables overhead, and if all was clear, I would push the rod back up and the six holes were drilled. "The war raged on."

* * * * *

The Japanese, Germans, and Italians had been preparing for war for years. America was just getting started. These carriers were desperately needed in all parts of the world. American's were dying for lack of equipment. Everything possible was being done to rush their delivery to the Navy. Every job throughout the ship was allotted a specific amount of money and time. If the crew doing the job completed the project early, the unspent dollars were divided among the crew. This was certainly an incentive to complete the work as early as possible. You could feel the sense of urgency every hour of the day, three eight hour shifts, twenty four hours a day, seven days a week. In a setting like this, safety was sure to be compromised. With hundreds of men working in very close quarters and large over head cranes carrying tons of equipment, our feet seldom touched the deck because of miles of uninstalled electrical cables and hoses that carried propane and oxygen for cutting torches and soldering, etc. At the age of fifteen I did not realize the possible danger all around me until what I am going to tell you now occurred.

One morning my first assignment was to locate the compartment directly below. The test hole was being drilled and usually, under working conditions, I had to go up to the hanger deck to find a passage way going down to the area I needed to find. This time the passage being used was located in the cradle (bottom) of the large elevator that lifts aircraft from the hanger deck to the flight deck. This is exactly as I remember more than sixty years later. I was just seconds from the passage and ladders going down into the ship when suddenly; there was a tremendous explosion two decks below. The force and debris coming straight up through that four by six foot hole looked like a cannon that had just fired a shell. Scaffolding and workers about thirty feet up, under the flight deck, scattered everywhere. I was stunned by the concussion but not hurt.

It seemed like only minutes passed before they started bringing up the mangled but covered bodies of the men killed. "The war raged on." This was only a tiny prelude to what was going to happen on this very deck in less than a year. I could see their feet sticking out from the bottom of the cover, their shoes and socks which they had put on less than two hours before, just as I had done. This burned a picture in my mind that I would never forget. I did a lot of growing up in a very short period of time. When the shock and confusion of the explosion was over, all workers were ordered back to work. A large compressed air tank had ruptured. I found another way to the compartment I was heading for when the explosion stopped me, pushed the welding rod back up, and the holes were drilled. It took me so long my work mates were wondering if I was one of those they carried off the ship. The impacted area was quickly secured and inspectors swarmed aboard. Sabotage was always suspected, findings were kept secret. If this were to happen today, nosy reporters with cameras and self serving politicians would swarm aboard hoping to point the finger of blame at someone and give our enemies valuable information.

* * * * *

This sleek, mighty, massive, complex, beautiful fighting machine was built in record time, only seventeen months from laying her keel to her commissioning. She was so eager to join the fight that during her launching ceremony, January 21, 1943, she began to slide down the ways minutes ahead of schedule but there was no stopping this behemoth. Her sponsor, First Lady Mrs. Eleanor Roosevelt, quickly broke the champagne bottle on her bow before she got away. She was involved in almost every battle in the Pacific until Tokyo Bay and earned the name "Fighting Lady". She later starred in a Hollywood film of that same name.

The aircraft carrier Yorktown, CV-10 is one of the few World War II Navy warships to survive the metal scrap heap. Since 1975, she is being restored and rests proudly in the Naval Museum, Patriots Point at Point Pleasant, South Carolina, near Charleston, for future generations to experience a tiny taste of what their grandfathers, fathers, brothers, and husbands did to protect the wonderful country and freedoms we have. Her size and mighty magnificence awes those who walk the same decks, in the very footprints of brave, young fighting men of World War II. Sailors and airmen from all parts of the free world were willing to give their lives if necessary, as hundreds did on this very ship that carried them directly to engage the enemy, vowing to destroy those who dare challenge their homeland. I urge veterans to take their children and grandchildren to visit the museum and watch movies of actual battles fought on the very ship you are on. Remember, at fifteen or sixteen years old, I helped build that ship. The theater you watch the movies in was built in the same elevator cradle as the explosion I experienced. Each year, hundreds of boy and girl scouts and other groups have the experience of spending days and sleeping nights aboard the carrier.

During the war there were five thousand plus Navy personnel living aboard this ship. While at the museum, be sure to visit the destroyer, "USS Laffey DD 724", known as the "ship that would not die." This is the same type of ships I served on for several years. While at the shipyard, I also helped build three other carriers that distinguished themselves during the war and following wars: The USS Hornet CV12, USS Franklin CV13, and the USS Intrepid CV II. All served courageously and succeeded in defeating a tough and committed enemy, the Japanese.

* * * * *

About four months before my seventeenth birthday, several of my Roanoke friends turned seventeen and went to the recruiting station to join the Navy. I decided to go with them and try to join. I got away with the shipyard at fifteen instead of sixteen. Maybe I could do it with the Navy, no luck, I would have to go back to Roanoke and get my parents signature stating that I was seventeen. "The war raged on." One of those who joined was later reported as missing at sea. He was never found. The time is now December 1943. The war has been going on for two years. This is the time I had been waiting for, my seventeenth birthday, December 22. I could now follow most of my friends into the military. I just could not wait to join the Navy.

I left the shipyard early in December and said goodbye to Mrs. Malnick. Only then did I learn that my mom was keeping up with me through telephone calls with Mrs. Malnick. It also answered how my older brother Al and a friend had suddenly showed up one day and explained some facts of life to me. I had met two older girls at a bowling alley; we bowled together, went to movies, and had dinner together with other friends. I noticed they would often go off with other guys, but they were just friends as far as I was concerned. Mrs. Malnick noticed something else and told mom about them. Soon, Al, my oldest brother, and his friend were on their way to Newport News to watch me for a while. That is when I learned another new word that in those days was not discussed in proper society. Prostitutes, yep, that is what they were, but they never displayed their wares to me, honest.

Most of my time after work was spent playing touch football or softball in a vacant lot nearby. Also movies, fishing, and to Buckroe Beach when the weather was warm with friends from back home or guys I worked with.

* * * * *

I packed and sent my belongings via Railway Express back home and for some reason decided to hitchhike, not a good idea. I had my last work pay in my pocket so it was not money, but another adventure that I would later tell my children was about to start. Keep in mind there were mostly narrow, two lane roads, not major highways, only routes winding through forests, farmland and every little town all the way. Motels were practically unheard of. Gas and oil were rationed. People drove no more than they had to, usually from home to work. No cars were being made and as if that were not enough, the bridge from Newport News across the James River to Smithfield was closed about three hours, making me way late getting started. I had two pluses in my favor, it was a warm sunny day and

Americans then were not afraid of each other. After the depression and during the war, men were always along the roadsides hitchhiking, many in uniform. People with cars and an extra seat would pick them up and carry them until they had to turn off the main road.

My next to last ride before dark was a very friendly older couple who dropped me off at a crossroads near their home. They were driving away when I discovered I had left my winter coat in the back seat of their car. This was December, the sun was going down and the temperature was dropping fast. About fifteen minutes later the couple returned with my coat. (My "angel" was there again.) In a few minutes the very next car stopped to give me a ride for about twenty miles. Again, I was let off at a lonely crossroads. It would soon be dark so I started walking. There would be no more cars until early morning. The moon was full and very bright but clouds were drifting by making it so dark I could barely see the road. No houses were in sight.

It was eerily quiet as I approached a wooded section on my right, up a small hill on a curve in the road. To my left was a vine covered fence and as I crested the hill I could see the white stones of an old country graveyard just beyond the fence. I began to hear very quiet, low moans. I could feel the hair on the back of my neck beginning to bristle and my breath becoming labored but there was nowhere to run, I had to keep on walking. Through small sections where there were no vines on the fence I could see farther into the darkness of the field and light morning fog or mist what appeared to be shimmering, floating white objects moving very slowly and the low, barely audible moans continued. The moonlight brightened and dimmed as the clouds passed by. I quickened my pace just short of running to get away from that place. I was sweating even though I was very cold. The woods to my right ended and a little farther ahead I could see the red embers of a smoldering fire. Again, I believe my "Guardian Angel" was watching over me. There was a big, old, rustic (spooky) sawmill, with a large, warmly inviting, smoldering at the bottom, ten foot pile of sawdust just waiting for me to take a stick, poke the ashes away, and release the warmth I desperately needed. The temperature was below freezing, frost all around me. To get to the sawmill I had to cross a railroad track; there was an empty boxcar sitting on a side rail. During the night, as I warmed up, I decided to go into the boxcar and maybe get a little sleep. I figured in this cold there could not be anything too dangerous in there. I had no flashlight so it was like walking into a strange, dark room. I found a wooden box to sit on, leaned back against the boxcar wall, and went to sleep.

Sometime later I was rudely and suddenly awakened by a terrifying noise. The whole boxcar lurched to one side; I felt like I was being sucked right out the door and just as suddenly the noise turned into a steady clatter and quickly it was gone. As my nerves calmed and my senses returned, I realized I had just experienced something that only hobos would understand, a huge, fast moving, thunderous, steam locomotive and freight train had just passed within two feet of where I was innocently sleeping. Somehow I was no longer sleepy but I was cold. I gladly returned to my own private sawdust pile, poked away the burnt ashes and bathed in the warmth coming from the red hot embers inside the pile. A car went by and I could now see lights inside a small farmhouse nestled in the trees across the road. I buttoned my coat, walked out to the road and waited. Soon a bus appeared around the curve where I had been scared out of my wits earlier. The bus was actually stopping for me, but before it did, it was now barely light enough for me to see into the field where I had heard the moaning and saw the ghosts earlier. The herd of white cows was still resting in the field, lowing the way cows do and the light fog was beginning to clear. Since cows do not scare me that much, I figure there just had to be a few real ghosts out there.

I had been on my feet most of the night so the bus seat was so comfortable and warm I quickly went to sleep. About forty-five minutes later the bus made a sharp left turn into the entrance to an army base and the driver said I would have to get off there. I was on a military bus and because I was wearing a tan, khaki colored coat, the driver picked me up because he thought I was an army soldier. "My angel again." Now I was back on the road again and it was starting a bright sunny day. The rides were longer and more often. Before nightfall I was in Roanoke and back home again to a good home cooked meal and a warm comfortable bed. I slept all night and most of the next day. That same day I went to the Navy recruiting office, picked up the papers I needed and because I was volunteering at seventeen, I had to have my parents' signature. They were now divorced; it took some persuading but they knew I was determined so each signed the papers. On my seventeenth birthday,

December 22, 1943, along with a group of other young men, I raised my right hand, repeated the oath of allegiance to defend my country against all enemies and was sworn into the Navy of the United States of America.

All of this did not go without incident and anxiety. During my physical examination one of the doctors noticed I had a slightly crooked left leg. The largest bone was broken when I was six years old and when the full plaster of Paris Leg Cast was removed they found my leg had healed a little bent. I guess Dr. Richards did the best he could with what he had to work with in 1932. However, I was able to convince the recruiting doctor that it had never been a problem. I was now officially a US Navy Sailor, in name only. A lot of learning and training lay ahead. "The war raged on."

* * * * *

Christmas was now in full swing. The Navy recruiting office was closed December 24th through 26th. I received orders to report to The Norfolk and Western Train Station on 27 December 1943 before departure time at 1540. Well now, I knew Norfolk and Western meant the N&W Train Station, I figured out they had put the day number before the month, but what was this 1540? I did not know until I called the recruiting office early December 27th. I was already being trained but did not know it.

I said my goodbyes to my family and met with a group of guys at the train station. We were told to bring personal items but no clothing except what we were wearing. The crowded train pulled out at 3:40 PM

(1540). I was off to a life filled with unbelievable adventure and to find and fall deeply in love and win the heart of a beautiful girl with whom I would spend the rest of my life. We were on our way to the Navy Training base at Bainbridge, Md. After a layover, changing trains in Petersburg, Va., we arrived at Bainbridge and twelve inches of snow, just in time for our first Navy meal. Every Friday beans were served for breakfast, cooked in a mildly sweet tasting, brown sugar broth? We kidded about it but I looked forward to and liked the beans breakfast.

There was a quick check by a doctor to see if we had any ailment that could spread to others. Next, in a room with a lot other guys, stripping down to our skivvies (shorts), putting all our clothes in a box to be shipped back home. Now we knew we were no longer civilians. We lined up in alphabetical order to be fitted with shoes and issued, not fitted, our G.I. uniforms, work clothes, underwear, socks, leggings, and white hats that did not fit. We were now called "Boots", and we were at boot camp. All Boots wore wrap around leggings over their pants leg just above the shoes to identify them as trainees. We were assigned to the lower section of one of many barracks on the sprawling training grounds. There were forty bunks, upper and lower on each wing of the barracks. Those of us who were assigned an upper bunk learned an extremely important lesson of what not to do. The thin sleeping pads would sometimes pull away from the railing edge of the bunk, leaving the wires and springs underneath exposed and when a man sits on the edge of his bunk bed, preparing to slide or jump to the floor, his male parts, we will call them "Family Jewels", tend to hang down into the springs. If you are not careful, before your feet hit the floor, you knew you forgot something very important. They were still up there in the springs. Thank goodness this didn't happen while I was there.

* * * * *

We were no longer individuals. We worked, trained, ate and slept together as a unit. We were company 3001. Reveille 0600 (6:00 AM), breakfast 0700, muster (roll call) and, flag raising 0800. This was our first full day to wear our new work clothes, white hats that didn't fit, blue shirts and dungarees with leggings. We were now officially boots. After the flag raising ceremony we began our basic schooling and familiarization classes, but there was a little something they had in store for us before that. We marched in formation for the first time. Only those of us who were "Boy Scouts" knew to start out on our left foot. There was some stumbling and yelling but they learned fast. We marched to a building and lined up in a long hallway. At the front of the line was a door with a large sign overhead, "BEAUTY PARLOR". We heard the screams, scuffling and gnashing of teeth as ten of us at a time were herded into that torture chamber where big burley, bald headed guys with long, hairy, tattooed arms holding dull sheep shears in their hands and a gleeful sneer on their face threw us into a barber chair, grabbed our hair in the back and removed every strand right down to the roots. There, on top of piles of black and red hair were my wavy, blonde locks that I had so carefully combed every strand every morning into place so the girls could oooh and ahh. Our heads nearly froze outside but at least we now understood why the "white hats we were issued were so small." Now they fit perfect. – On a second reading of the above, I guess I did get a bit carried away and exaggerated just a little bit. But on a more serious side, we later heard rumors and learned that perhaps at this very same time, men, women, and children in Europe were having their hair shaved too. But it was being used to stuff truck, tank seats, etc so the Germans could sit more comfortable. This was the beginning of many ten hour training days. Evening meal 1800 hours (6 PM), taps, lights out 2200 hours (10 PM).

* * * * *

"The war raged on." Now into the third year, a lot of training was crammed into six weeks of boot camp. I will tell you a few of the more humorous experiences. Boys will be boys, and in every branch of the military there are practical jokes to be played on the new guys. Such as sending him to find a "steam strainer", a left-handed "monkey wrench" or a "sky hook" to name a few. Raw recruits were fair game, we all were victims at some time or other. We were beginning to hear rumors of shot day, a series of immunity shots, including one with a long square needle in the left testical. (Sorry but there is not a nice way to say it). We were all dreading that day but it did come.

By this time we were wearing our "Undress Blues", an informal blue uniform worn when performing routine office work, attending classes, etc, not performing manual labor. We were lined up between tables in the mess hall, two lines. At the front of each line were four new, practicing young corpsmen sitting on tables, two on each side of the lines with boxes of needles and serum. Keep in mind, this was January 1944, needles were not refined down to the tiny hair size like today, they were all the same size, long and thick. We wondered about the pillows stacked on a nearby table. We were told to pull off our jackets, "The top part of a Navy uniform has no buttons or zippers, you must put your arms into the sleeves and pull it over your head." The line began to move, we soon found the reason for the pillows, some didn't even make it to the needles before they passed out. I think most of the guys were like me, I had never had a shot before. I made it thru the needles but I have to admit, I had to sit down and put my head between my knees for a while. "Oh boy", now I have to pull that jacket back over my head, this time it wasn't so bad, we were told to exercise our arms all during the day.

It was a long night and we got very little sleep. The aspirin we were given may have helped some; a hot shower helped but the hot water soon ran out. When morning came we were really a pitiful sight trying to put our clothes on, luckily we were wearing regular work shirts but had to help each other get dressed. We were sore but our training had to go on. "Oh" by the way, that long, square needle I mentioned earlier didn't happen, it was just some "dum dum's" way of having fun, scaring new recruits. Come to think of it, I do believe we did mention it to some new guys who came in after us but we only told one, course he told others and the news spread rapidly.

* * * * *

"The war raged on." We were constantly reminded of the seriousness of why we were being trained. Many of us could soon be in kill or be killed situations. We were taught to hate our enemies so when the time came we could do what had to be done to survive. I am only sharing with you in this writing some of the more humorous parts of that training. Such as the day we experienced what it was like to be gassed. And I don't mean the kind you pass after beans for breakfast. We were lined up outside a building with no windows, about the size of a large garage that would hold 30 of us at a time. Since we would be in the first group to go in, a couple of my buddies and I sized up the situation, if we were last in we would be first out when the door opened. Pretty smart thinking, we had no gas masks. We heard the door being bolted behind us, in came the gas, our nose and eyes were burning, hard to breathe, tears were pouring from our eyes. When are they going to open that door? We began to panic, suddenly my buddies and I realized our mistake, the building had two doors. The other was at the far opposite corner. We were last in, last out; the instructors were yelling, "open your eyes wide," let the wind blow the gas out, we had been tear gassed. I won't mention any names but the instructors had a big belly laugh watching certain guys maneuvering around to be last in first out, <u>emba</u>rrassing.

* * * * *

I am not sure the exact date we departed boot camp, sometime last of February 1944, there was twelve or more inches of snow on the ground at Bainbridge Md. I was one of what was considered, the lucky ones, again, "my Guardian Angel" and what I feel was a part of God's intricate plan for me to find my Katherine at the exact right time in each of our lives. My group was to be dispersed to several Navy air bases in Florida. Most of the others were sent to northern and southern California, many were assigned to Pacific Fleet ships. The Pacific Ocean naval, air, and sea battles with the Japanese and invading the south Pacific islands were at their highest point. Some of the greatest naval battles in history, before or after WWII were now going on. Some of those I trained with at Bainbridge did not come back, some not even making it to their eighteenth birthday.

None in my group had ever been to Florida so when we received the good news, visions of girls, palm trees, girls, warm sandy beaches, girls, balmy sunsets, and girls in bathing suits danced in our imaginations and dreams. We were now full fledged, raw boots, fresh out of boot camp and ready to conquer the world. Our hair was beginning to grow back. We were in uniform and expected to be treated royally. Our royal train was waiting for us, box cars, like they put horses and cattle in, but they had remodeled these cars, cut holes in the sides for big picture windows, built in bunks, plumbing, I can't remember having lights but there really wasn't any straw on the floor. This was to be our home for the three days it took from Maryland to Florida. It's funny, I can't remember having even one meal during that trip. For every regular troop train going north or south we were pulled onto a side rail to wait for it to pass. We began to see what we thought were palm trees going by and we figured as soon as we crossed that Florida line it would be summertime. Well, somebody sure been tellin' lies! We stopped for some of the guys getting off at the Jacksonville Naval

Air Station and it was colder than Bainbridge. Another twenty minute ride to my groups stop, and as we were being herded off the train somebody yelled, "Hey there's nothing out here!"

The time was about three o'clock in the morning, dark and cold. The train started rolling and quickly disappeared into the night. There we were with our sea bags packed tight and heavy beside the tracks with nothing but swamp land on either side. We could see a single light about a half mile back up the tracks; the engineer had overshot our royal plush passenger station. When we finally arrived at our royal plush passenger station destination, it was about the size of a three hole out house with a little roof and a short board seat, no holes. We were fascinated by the lonesome, little, single light. In the pitch dark night we could see no houses or buildings nearby and we could not see any electric wires leading to the little shack. It was sure nice to warm our hands. We were also thankful it wasn't raining. This place was beginning to get a little spooky, light burning without wires. We were afraid to move about too much 'cause we could surprise a cotton mouth or something else out of that swamp. The little shack was sitting exactly on the end of the road and we figured that Greyhound bus they would surely send for us may not stop in time. We also began to figure this may be a big joke to test our sense of humor, or maybe they wanted to see if we learned anything during our island survival training. Suddenly, the whole place lit up from a pair of bright lights coming down the dirt road. The Navy driver of the station wagon apologized profusely, saying this was his first time to find this place and he got lost. He was also afraid his body might be found later in the swamp. We were about a fifteen minute ride from the naval air station at Green Cove Springs, Fl. We spent what was left of the night in a temporary sleeping quarters.

Reveille at 0700, we had about three hours sleep. After the morning meal (no beans), we were officially checked in as base personnel and received our job assignments and barracks living quarters. That means one clothes locker and an upper bunk to sleep on along with 79 other guys in one upper wing of the building. By this time I was used to this type of living. We were "raw boots" because our hair was just beginning to grow out again. I came to like this small air base but it was not what I really wanted. During my first month, I started filling in the papers requesting reassignment to sea duty, preferably aboard the Navy fighting ships called Destroyers. More about that later.

* * * * *

I learned the reason why we were dumped off the train in the middle of a swamp. They were working on the tracks at the small Green Cove Springs station. The tracks were torn up, our train came down other tracks and that little shack was close to the base, being used temporarily. This air station received new pilots after they had completed their basic flight training. Here they would fly for the first time, the actual fighter plane they would be flying into combat. There were two types of single pilot air craft on this airfield, eighty of each, Grummond – F4F Wildcats and Vought – F4U Corsairs. At the beginning of the war the stubby, fat, little Wildcat was the hottest fighter plane the Navy had, others came later. The Corsair was a marine fighter plane used by the Navy because it was an excellent aircraft carrier plane, had beautiful features, and was called the flying cigar because of the fuselage shape and the gull shaped wings, a later design aircraft than the Wildcat.

Again, my "Guardian Angel". Being a second class seaman, of all the menial jobs I could have received, I just couldn't believe I was assigned to work directly with the planes. Each aircraft had a plane captain. This was a trained enlisted man who was responsible for everything his plane needed from early morning until tie down time each night. He was there every morning one hour before the pilots came out, to take the tie down lines off, check all control surfaces, start the engine for warm-up, and check in flight instrument panel controls, fuel, oil, oxygen bottle. When the pilot came to my plane he was only a little older than me. I assisted him getting into the seat and to properly buckle up, the parachute he wore also served as his seat cushion. I plugged in his oxygen line, wished him a good flight, jumped off the wing, pulled the wheel chocks, walked to the front of the plane where the pilot could see me clearly, and gave the thumbs up signal, all clear to start the engine. When the pilot receives radio clearance to move out, he cannot see in front of his plane because these had a tail wheel, making the front of the plane higher than the pilot. With the huge three bladed propeller turning he must rely on his plane captain, with special signals to guide him safely between other planes to the taxi strip. After that he is on his own in a line of planes to the takeoff runway. Most of us would climb up on other planes to watch the takeoffs, especially when there were student pilots flying this type of aircraft for their first time.

There were many exciting moments, also tragic ones. Powerful engines, new pilots. The first time I actually witnessed a man die. He gave full throttle to gain flying speed, suddenly his plane veered sharply to the left and smashed into a large cement block holding a runway flood light. The tank was filled with high octane fuel and it burst into flames before rescue vehicles arrived. We could see the young pilot, 21-23 years old, like many of us. He was slumped over, either unconscious or killed by the impact. He did not feel the flames and nothing could be done to save him. It was a somber ground crew that day. This was not what we wanted to see. "The war raged on," another telegram with a star on the envelope. Later it was determined a careless plane captain had failed to remove the "rudder batten", used to keep the rudder secured from wind overnight. The aircraft could not be controlled. The investigating committee reported ninety percent pilot and ten percent plane captain error. The pilot is supposed to visually inspect all control surfaces, also he taxied a tenth of a mile without properly testing his flight controls.

There are many jobs in an operation like that. Mechanics in the large hanger, truck drivers to take fuel and oil to the planes, trouble shooters to drive pickups with air compressors, etc for filling and changing tires, radio communications men and many others but for some reason, I was assigned what, to me, was the dream job of being trained to be a "Plane Captain". Muster is a military term for assembling a particular group of men to determine if all are present or accounted for, such as "plane captains" and trainees.

* * * * *

Every aircraft on the base was numbered and painted in camouflage colors of blue and grey except one, I couldn't help but notice it every day. It was unpainted and all silver, stainless steel; the number on it was #1. It stood out from every other plane on the base. Three weeks later when my name was called during early muster, I was told to report to the chief's office. He told me I had qualified to be a "Plane Captain". When he checked his list he said, "Well, aren't you lucky, you've got #1." "My Guardian Angel again." Being a plane captain was enough, but when he said #1, I nearly exploded, tears came to my eyes. The chief said, "Well, if you're gonna cry about it I'll see if another one will soon be open." Then, he laughed, threw me some wipe rags and said, "Go start making her shine." The chief and I became good friends. Standard equipment for a plane captain was a wipe rag, a screwdriver for opening the different compartments, and a special tool to twist and clip small safety wires. When I walked out and looked at "my beautiful, Silver Lady", I was so excited I just wanted to scream, but I had a job to do before the pilots arrived. I also learned the higher ranking flight commanders usually flew #1, it was different.

When I started taking the tie down lines off, plane captains nearby yelled, asking me if I really got #1? We didn't have time to talk then, the fuel truck pulled up; I filled the tank and checked the oil. When I slid the canopy back, climbed into the cockpit and lowered myself into the seat, it was like a dream come true. I just sat there a few minutes trying to accept the reality that "here I am, just seventeen and totally in command of a real U.S. Navy Fighter Plane". My name would soon be painted on the side just below the canopy. "W. M. Hillman – Plane Captain." Oh, I knew I was only a caretaker, a seaman 2nd class, the lowest of the lowest, but I also knew if I found something wrong and put the plane on the "No Fly list", even the base commander could not override my order until it was checked out. "So there."

I came back to reality, now it was time to start that big engine for my first time. I had learned to start other engines just like it but this one was mine. I got the thumbs up, all clear signal from a helper outside. Brakes on, I flipped the switch to fire the cartridge that made the engine turn over and start. The "F4F Wildcat" did not use a battery assisted mechanism to start the engine. A cartridge in a breech, like you would use to fire a shotgun was used. This was an exhilarating moment for me, I could see the big three bladed propeller begin to turn as it came to life and began to purr smoothly. In the warm-up I could feel the power, it seemed to be saying, turn me loose, let me pull this plane high above the earth and soar over 300 mph, remember, its 1944.

I named my plane after my kid sister. "Jeannie", was painted on each side of the engine cowling. When the pilots returned from training flights, the plane captains were waiting to safely guide them to their tie down spot. When the planes were on the ground and taxiing in, someone would yell the name or the number. Several nights a week the pilots were trained to fly at night. This included takeoffs, landings, cross country, formation flying, etc. This of course included the ground crew. Some were stationed at the start of the incoming runway. Sometimes the busy, new pilots would forget to lower their landing gear. The ground crew had lights to spot this little oversight and would treat them to a fireworks display of bright flares. The surprised and startled new pilots would have to gun their engine to gain flying speed and get in line again for their landing and a royal chewing out from his flight commander. Several times I watched them continue to land after the flares were fired. Then, they were the ones treating us to the fireworks when the shower of sparks sprayed from the wings or belly of the plane, a wheels-up landing, embarrassing. They each thought the flares were for the plane behind them.

* * * * *

Each night the duty cooks had to send sandwiches and coffee to the ground crew. One time, four nights straight, they sent only marmalade sandwiches. On the fourth night every crewman threw the marmalade back into the boxes, we grabbed bolt cutters and went to the mess hall, cut the locks, dumped the marmalade sandwiches on the floor of the galley for the cooks to pick up, found cooked hams and other meats and had ourselves a feast before the base M. P.'s showed up. We far outnumbered them so they decided to just make a report. We had a better variety of sandwiches after that, but we did look closely inside of them for a while. Oh, I almost forgot the M.Ps sat down and ate with us; everybody was laughing except the cooks the next morning, and the mess hall chief. We heard the chief was trying to get as many names as he could to put on report for breaking into the mess hall. It ended up with the chief in trouble for causing the problem. The incident was named, "The Great Marmalade Raid".

* * * * *

I made some very good friends while I was there. One was my bunk mate, I had the upper bunk, he had the lower; he was a third class petty officer from Coral Gables Fl. He taught me a lot about the job I had, that's how I became a plane captain so quickly. The base had a limited number of qualified taxi pilots, he was one of them, that means he started the engine and moved or taxied the plane on the ground to wherever it had to be taken on the base, for instance, way across the runways to the firing range to have the 50 caliber machine guns checked. He taught me how to taxi the planes and I became a qualified taxi pilot, which I really enjoyed. He was also the first person to call me "Wally instead of Wallace". As you know, the nickname stuck. His name is John Frances Witcher, thanks Johnny.

* * * * *

Now for the job I did not like, I had to serve for a while on the recovery team for accidents, crashes, etc. These types of fighter planes had very limited gliding ability, if the engine stalled or cut out the pilot had to put the plane into a steady controlled decent to maintain flying speed and try to spot a field to put it down. If this happened during night flying, the pilot's only chance was to bail out. If he was at low altitude and stalled, the heavy engine would pull it straight down like a rock. When this happened the recovery team had to bring out whatever remained, usually this was on swampy and or wooded areas and we had to cut trees to form enough of a bed to bring in a treaded vehicle. The cotton mouths and gators really loved this. It seemed like every time we had an especially messy – grizzly one to clean up, the mess cooks were notified to serve spaghetti or some other dish with a lot of red tomatoes and other stuff (think about it). The regular "Recovery Team guys" wanted us to think you get use to it, but when we talked to them one on one they admitted they never really got hardened to what they had to do. They learned just not to think about it after the job was finished.

    I will share with you the saddest and most unusual crash site I helped with. The plane had come down during the night training into a swamp several hundred feet from a dry land fire trail. We had to cut trees to hold the metal road bed sections for the (I believe it was called a tram) tank type treads that could lift out the heavy parts of the plane if needed. It had come straight down leaving a hole about twenty feet diameter filled with murky swamp water, only parts of the wings could be seen. Using special grappling hooks we had pulled out parts of the tail section when we noticed a male civilian making his way over the road bed. It was the father of the young pilot. He lived in a nearby city and somehow had learned of the crash. He refused to leave until he – himself had identified his son. We had to continue, we had removed the tail section and most of the fuselage including parts of the cockpit. Next, should be or contain body parts, we knew this. The father was out of the way, standing nearby. We had our job to do but this was the first time a parent was present and watching our every move. We also knew what was likely coming next, we probed until we found something soft, it was part of the pilot's flight suit but not the part with his name or anything recognizable. Later came a shoe and foot, he asked us to remove the shoe – one toe was deformed. We didn't have to be told, it was his son. Every man, including the old timers had to turn away with our hands over our faces as the father made his way back to his car. We all agreed this one we would remember for the rest of our lives.

There were others, I shared this one with you only because it was unusual in a special way. Normally, when we walked away from the crash site, our part was over. This time, like it or not, we were involved in the toughest part, the family. Even the base commander and chaplain said they had never heard of anything like this.

* * * * *

"Rosie," ah yes, now I'll tell you about my little "Rosie". The air base derived its name, "Green Cove", from a very small but quaint picturesque town called Green Cove Springs, Florida. Spanish moss covered trees lined the streets. One theater, several small restaurants, etc. All larger cities, where the base personnel would go, were about forty-five minutes to an hour away, like St. Augustine, Jacksonville, or Palatka where we would go to beaches, fun places, etc. The air base had a small theater with movies every night. On the base was about thirty young women who were WAVES. (Women Accepted Volunteer Emergency Services) They worked mostly in the offices and sick bay (hospitals). Those of us working in the aviation section saw them usually, only at the movie. The doors were not opened until about ten minutes before the movies started, so if you wanted a seat you arrived early. In those days, chivalry was still practiced. – I think you girls of today are pretty dumb to let the radical feminists take this away from you. Guys would treat you like ladies if you would let them know you expect to be treated like a special lady, try it. Make them open doors for you. – The WAVES were let in first and they would gather outside the door in a group.

One night, I was standing next to the WAVES; they were all laughing and talking when I heard loudly, the cutest, most infectious giggle and laugh I had ever heard. It made me feel good and want to laugh, but I could not see her. I asked one of the girls to point her out to me. All the other girls were taller and in the middle was a little Jewish girl, barely tall enough to qualify for the WAVES. Then, the door opened, the ladies went in first and would sit in a group, us guys would scramble for seats or have to stand. The next night I was a little late and was walking to a place to stand with other guys. I noticed some of the girls seemed to be looking at me when a girl sitting next to the isle reached out and took my hand. The girl in the next seat got up and went to another. The one holding my hand said, "This is your seat, sit down, I want to introduce you to Rosie." I was flabbergasted to say the least, (whatever that means). I told Rosie my name and in her smiley voice she said, "Well, hi Wally, nice to meet you," and shook my hand. I was glad the lights were dimmed and the movie started so I could get the bewildered look off my face. By the end of the movie we had talked a little and I walked with her to her barracks.

The very next night when I went in for the movie, I heard some of the girls say, "He's here, he's here!" and the same thing happened. The next two nights I was on duty, the third night when I went in, some of the girls were looking back for me and said, "Wally, there's a seat for you next to Rosie." When I sat down, I noticed some dirty looks from the guys standing up. That night I asked Rosie to have dinner with me in town and go to a movie.

Saturday evening, I walked to the WAVES barracks a little early, I had never been there. I walked into a little entrance sitting room and I heard that, "He's here," again. About ten minutes later Rosie walked in with three other girls, they were her roommates. It was as though they were presenting her to me for my approval. Rosie's brown hair was no longer up under her uniform cap; it was down to her shoulders, shiny and wavy, high heels (a little taller) and makeup. I sensed what was going on and hoped I reacted the way they wanted, but I was only seventeen and a shy guy too. The girls were still putting every hair in place as we went out the door. I said, "They must like you a lot." She told me they had been like old mother hens, fussing with her hair and makeup, and telling her what to say all afternoon. Rosie was really not pretty, she was cute!

We took a Navy bus to Green Cove and walked to a nice little restaurant with low lights and candles on the tables. We were talking while waiting for our food to be served when Rosie stopped talking and became very quiet. When she looked up at me, she said,

"Wally, you could have had any one of the other girls that you wanted, they are all prettier than me. Why did you choose me?" I held her hand and said, "Rosie, you have something the other girls will never have, your sense of humor and that squeaky, delightful, friendly laughter of yours is what got my attention. It made me feel good, and besides, in your own way, I think you are just as pretty as any of the other girls." Tears came into her eyes and she said, "Wally, you are the first boy I have ever been out with." Now, I understood why her roommates had been fussing over her and coaching her all afternoon. But they didn't tell her to say this, it was straight from her heart. I believe I gave her her first kiss that night.

"The war raged on," military personnel were subject to immediate transfer if necessary. Monday and Tuesday I was on night flight duty. When I went to the movie Wednesday night, the girls told me Rosie had been sent to Europe Sunday. Rosie was a nurse, she had been sent immediately to where she was needed. She had tried to get a message to me but didn't have time. I never saw or heard from Rosie again. I hope she made it through the war. Somehow, I feel like I made a difference in her life. One of her friends who worked in the personnel office pulled my records and told Rosie all about me, she was two years older than me. I thought about my little Rosie for a long time but only as a new friend.

* * * * *

"Once again my "Guardian Angel" was there for me. A group of my buddies and I decided to go to Jacksonville for some fun. We were just seventeen year old kids looking for something to get into. We took in a movie, then we heard about some strip joints, none of us had been to a strip joint so we decided to see if what we had heard was true. We all walked in, they checked our I.D.'s, we all walked out, didn't see nothin, too young. One of the guys was just old enough to buy whiskey so we all chipped in for a couple of bottles. Just then I felt a hand on my shoulder, it was a first class petty officer from our base who had helped me when I was learning to be a "Plane Captain". A big, square jawed type of fellow, he said come on with me, I know of a bar where we can get some really good drinks. He took me to a juice bar and we had tropical fruit juice and ice cream and went to a mariner's museum. When I saw the other guys Monday morning some of them were still sick. Yep, my "angel" took me right out of that group.

* * * * *

On the air base there were church services during the week and of course on Sunday. All my younger life the church was the center of activity. Dad and mom took us kids twice on Sunday, Wednesday nights, and other times for special activities. We were brought up in the church. This carried over into my teen years in the Navy. In Green Cove Springs there was a small chapel that I liked and attended when I could go. The first time I visited this chapel, unknown to me, they had sent a post card to my dad telling him, "Your son Wallace attended church services in our chapel, he did not sit in the back, he came right down to the front and actively participated. We are very proud of him as we know you are." I didn't know anything about this until after my dad passed away, he had been carrying the card in his billfold, all those years.

* * * * *

When our assigned plane was in the air, sometimes we had special training. We had about three hours to do just about anything we wanted to, sleep – goof off, go to the commissary for milkshakes, study our training manuals, just as long as we were there when our planes came back. One day I noticed a jeep that had been sitting in back of our line shack for several days. The keys were in the ignition, I sat down in the driver's seat for a while, studying the controls. I was a qualified taxi pilot but I didn't know how to drive a car. I decided that was going to change, forgetting that cars have clutches and gears, planes don't. I turned the ignition key, the jeep, in gear, lurched forward, lesson #1, lucky there was nothing in front. There was a short paved driveway about the length of a football field leading to the officers' quarters. Lesson #2, I pushed in the clutch, turned on the engine and held on for dear life as I let the clutch out too fast, that jeep bucked and jumped like a wild bucking horse with a new rider. The engine stalled. I started the engine again, let the clutch out slower, it bucked a few times but smoothed out. I was driving for my first time!

    I came to the end of the road, no place to turn around. Here we go again, finally found reverse gear, oops, same thing going backwards. I finally got it turned around, "on the road again." I had my own little road, no other cars to bother me or bump into. On my third trip it happened. I had turned around, suddenly, I was surrounded by six pilots who had just returned from a training flight and wanted a ride to their barracks at the other end of my little road. They were sitting on the hood, in the seats, and one hanging onto the spare tire. I got nervous, let the clutch out too fast, and the ones on the hood slid back against the windshield. The others grabbed whatever was handy; I don't know what happened to the one on the spare tire. These guys had just returned from gunnery and air combat practice from fifteen thousand feet up. I didn't have to tell them I was learning to drive. They thanked me for the ride and one quipped, "That was the most exciting part of our day."

* * * * *

After four days of practicing between flights, I had it all down pretty good. Then, whoever parked the jeep drove it away. After that I drove whenever I got the chance. My best friend on the base owned a car and he would let me drive when we went to one of the nearby cities during our weekends off. Once, when I had taxied a plane to the firing range, across runways to the far side of the base, there was no one there to bring me back but there was a jeep I could use. The jeep was parked close to a plane so I had to back it up one of the dirt mounds used to fire bullets into. The jeeps are four wheel drive, suddenly the wheels on the right side dug deeply into softer dirt. The jeep was starting to roll over as I climbed out. Luckily, the windshield on those jeeps could be laid down flat on the hood so no damage was done but the jeep was upside down. All the guys came over and we rolled it back on its wheels. I got back in and drove away, yuk, yuk, yuk. Teaching myself to drive would later prove to be very important in a way I could never have dreamed of.

* * * * *

During our time while our plane was in the air, a few of us decided to start studying for our third class petty officer rating. Since we were involved in aviation at the time, we checked out the manuals for aviation mechanic. I studied but my heart really was not in it. Seven of us took the test together, when the results came in, five of the seven had passed. I was one of them; we received our petty officer stripe and insignia and proudly sewed them on our uniform sleeve. Two weeks later we were told a clerical error had been made. Five of us did not pass, including me. The two who were told they had failed were the two who actually had passed. Off came our stripe, we received some kidding about this but somehow it didn't bother me too much. I just didn't want to be a mechanic and assigned to an aircraft carrier. I put in another request for destroyer duty.

* * * * *

I had never really thought about the day coming that I would sadly learn that anything mechanical is subject to failure, nothing man made will last forever. Nothing unusual, wakeup call 0600, morning meal at mess hall, muster 0700, performed all plane captain duties as described previously, pilots arrived 0800, and the <u>flight leader</u> took # 1 "Jeannie". I wished him a good flight, jumped off the wing as I had done hundreds of times, watched the takeoffs, and went with other PC's to the ships store lunch counter for a second cup of coffee and probably donuts. The base chapel was in the same building and the chaplain had some type of program which we attended and then played ping-pong for a while before returning to our line shack in which there was a radio receiver that we could hear pilots talking with each other during in flight training, sometimes it got really exciting. This time, there was a frantic "May Day – May Day" call, the pilot yelled his plane was going down in a wide spiral and would not respond to controls. His final transmission was, "I'm bailing out, I'm bailing out!" Other pilots came on giving their position and reporting their flight leader (I froze) was in parachute and the plane had hit the water, it was # 1, I was shocked! I could not believe what I had just heard.

  The next transmission that I did hear was that a fast P.T. boat was on the way to pick up the pilot. #1 was gone forever, in the Atlantic Ocean, somewhere off the coast from St. Augustine, Florida area. My name is on each side of the cockpit and Jeannie's name on each side of the engine cowling. Possible cause, a control cable to the wing ailerons snapped; something the plane captain could not inspect completely. The pilot was rescued, he came by the next day, told me he was sorry he lost my plane and explained what happened. A replacement F4F Wildcat was brought in, it was newer but the same camouflage color as all the other Wildcats. I took good care of it but I could not become as attached to it like I was with my "Jeannie". I talked with the chief of "Plane Captains", told him I would like to learn more about the "F4U Corsairs" and requested "Plane Captain" positions on a Corsair.

  About two weeks later, I got my request. Corsairs were a much larger, later and different design fighter plane. I no longer had to put a shotgun cartridge into a breech and fire it every time the engine was started. I simply pushed the starter switch and the battery supplied the power to make that huge, three bladed propeller, even larger than the Wildcats, start turning. It only took a few days for me to learn all I needed to know to take charge of my Corsair, and yes, the Navy Air Corps soon had a Corsair named "Jeannie".

* * * * *

USO – United Service Organization – many of you have heard of this voluntary group of people all over the world who did a wonderful job of entertaining and bringing a little bit of a feeling of hometown, relaxing atmosphere to military personnel in almost every part of the world. Most every larger city near military areas had a USO club. These clubs were well organized and strictly supervised. All, in uniform military, were welcomed with open arms to pleasant, homelike, clean surroundings with friendly people. Alcohol was strictly forbidden and snack food always available. For the most part, these were places where married men and guys who had sweethearts back home could enjoy dancing with and having female companionship for an evening and still be faithful and true to those who trusted and were waiting for them back home.

During those times, even in close knit, Bible belt communities, it was acceptable for the young women to go to planned USO dances and parties because they were supervised and the girls were not allowed to "pair off, leave with, or make dates" with the guys. But mother nature ignores man made rules. Many long term successful marriages started with two young people meeting at the USO club. Each knew the other did not hang out at bars or dance halls where men went to pick up women. I have only good things to say about the USO. Bob Hope is a perfect example of those associated with the USO. Even to our little Green Cove Air Base, the USO brought well know "big bands" and entertainment to us several times. The big airplane hanger was cleaned up and we had some great dances there. I don't know where all the girls came from but that is where I learned to enjoy dancing. The WAVES, on the base, normally dressed in work clothes and hair in a bun or tucked under their caps. Suddenly, they were pretty young ladies in heels, skirts, and wavy hair down to their shoulders.

* * * * *

Often, during my free time at the Green Cove Air Base, I enjoyed learning other duty work. I had a friend who worked in the ordinance gang taking care of ammunition, all types of firearms but especially the 50 caliber machine guns in the fighter planes' wings. When those planes went on a training flight to practice "dog fighting", they were firing their guns at a long, round, funnel shaped target so the air could pass through. It was about twenty feet long, made of the same type of white material that parachutes are made of. The target is towed on a line about 500 feet behind another plane. Before loading the four wing guns with long belts of 50 caliber machine gun bullets, the tips of the bullets are dipped in special slow drying paint. A recorded color for each plane so the pilots and their squadron leader could see who did and did not hit the target.

I wanted to watch how they got the target behind the plane. Five of us in a jeep drove out to the beginning of a runway where one guy got out and tied the tow line to a secure ring in the ground. The other four of us drove away with line feeding off a large spool until all the line was on the ground. They brought out the target, about as big around as an average garbage can. They <u>showed</u> me how they secure the tow line to the target, they <u>showed</u> me how they hold the target up high, and they <u>showed</u> me how they would stand so the tow line would not loop around their ankles. They <u>told</u> me when the plane reached the target holder the pilot would pull up into a steep climb, they <u>told</u> me the curve in the line comes at them about 150 miles an hour and if all goes well the target is lifted right out of their hands. All this time I was the one holding the target and out of the corner of my eye I could see one of them waving hand signals. All three jumped in the jeep and took off. "What a revoltin' development this is," somebody been playin' a game of "<u>show</u> and <u>told</u>". I had never been this close to the runway while a plane was taking off. Suddenly, I heard a deafening roar, here it comes, full throttle, straight at me, that propeller looked big as a windmill. Now let's see, how am I supposed to stand? Sometimes I learned fast, that plane seemed close enough I could spit on it, the pilot and I looked at each other, it was all over in seconds and the plane and target disappeared. Those guys thought it was funny but it was something they did every day. I had to laugh too and it was all over so quickly I didn't have time to really get scared. Later, one of them told me about the time the tow line behind the plane snagged on something on the runway causing a loop that nearly wrapped around his ankles. Well, like I always say, I'll try most anything once.

* * * * *

I really enjoyed my time at Green Cove Air Base, a great learning experience and time for me to gradually ease into military life. Early December 1944, several of us were called to the P.C. chief's office and received the news that we would be shipping out in two days. We packed our sea bags, said goodbye to friends, and were on a bus for temporary duty at Naval Air Station, Jacksonville, Florida, where we were assigned into barracks with about seventy-five other sailors awaiting transfers. The next morning we were assembled outside the barracks and as our names were called we were assigned to one of three groups for work details. Now this time I don't know if my angel was with me or if a little devil was sitting on my shoulder, but my name was never called. I just slipped into the nearest group. By now I had learned to never volunteer for anything (except maybe to inspect the WAVES barracks) unless the chief points and tells you that you are a volunteer.

In the Navy, in order to pass through a guarded gate or leave the ship you must have an authorized gate pass called a "Liberty Card". They started handing out Liberty Cards to all in the work details and when they didn't call my name I said, "Hey, where's my Liberty Card?" By now the detail busses were waiting. I told him my name and he ran back to the barracks office and made one for me. I had a gate pass, now all I needed was a job. I went back into the barracks, put my uniform on, my work clothes in a bag, went out the main gate on a bus going into town, and went to the

"Railway Express Agency", (like U.P.S. today), I heard they were hiring. I got me a paying job loading and unloading railroad freight cars of baskets of tropical fruit, etc. going north for the Christmas season. I now knew I would not make it home for Christmas and I needed extra money to send gifts. I did this for several weeks until I noticed others starting to leave. The guy in the office was a seaman like me so I didn't worry too much about him. I asked him if he could tell me when and where I would be going. I told him my name, he said, "I've been lookin' for you, where the heck have you been?" I told him, "Like everyone else, I've been workin'." (See, I didn't tell a fib.) Now I knew where, but most important when I would be leaving. So the next morning I went to work, this was a temporary job and we were paid each day for as many hours as we could work. I have no idea why my name was left off the original list and I didn't ask. Soon I was on the next temporary, but longer leg of my journey. A six month, temporary assignment here, would form the absolute pinnacle of my four year Navy career and the key to winning the heart of the wonderful lady who would become the mother of my children and loving, faithful, devoted partner for life and I hope and pray, eternity.

* * * * *

St. Simons Island, Georgia, located off the coast from Brunswick, Georgia, several miles from the air base, the Navy had acquired a small yacht club. Planes taking off at the base were over the Atlantic Ocean. Occasionally, there were engine failures or other problems causing the planes to go down into the water. The yacht club was used to base three, stripped down, powerful patrol torpedo boats, (PT boats). Each day these boats were assigned a position in the ocean to quickly rescue crews and passengers from downed planes. On bad weather days we also helped the coast guard look for and retrieve bodies known to be in the water. The ten miles to the city of Brunswick had three long bridges with thick wooden planks for a road bed, the planks made quite a rhythmic clatter when cars drove over them. During the short time I was there, several drivers either missed the bridge or found a way to drive off of them, alcohol probably helped them accomplish this. Their bodies were found weeks later.

I really enjoyed my duty at the yacht club. The enlisted men had a small barracks and the few officers had living quarters in the club building. We had our own cook and ate in the club dining room, we enjoyed fishing, had pool and ping pong tables, etc., even the U.S.O. would send people with a truck full of games to entertain us. When we went to Brunswick for a short Liberty we just walked down the driveway to the road and soon people driving by would stop and pick us up. One Friday evening I was by myself, in dress uniform, waiting for a ride as I had many times before, when around the curve came a big, shiny limousine, it stopped for me. I was about to experience a piece of history that few people could even imagine. The door popped open, a big, burly sergeant with a booming voice, a chest full of medals and hash marks up his sleeve said, "Hop in sailor, do you know your way around this area?" This limousine had sirens, special locks on the doors, and radio equipment like I had never seen. I was so busy looking that I must have hesitated, the sarge laughed and said, "Don't worry, it affects everybody like that when they first see it. This is General Eisenhower's personal limousine and I am his chauffeur, body guard, and personal aide. The general just returned from Europe and is getting some R & R (rest and relaxation) with his wife, Mamie, at the Cloister Hotel and Resort on Jeckle Island. He gave me the weekend off and I'm looking for someone who knows their way around this area. You're a sailor, you know what I'm looking for, come on just show me what this place has to offer."

* * * * *

Personal note: Five Star General Dwight D. Eisenhower (later President) was then the absolute supreme, Allied Commander of Troops in the European Theater. He personally gave the order for the largest expeditionary force ever assembled on earth on June 6, 1944, to begin the invasion of Europe and the eventual downfall of Hitler and the German Military. General Eisenhower and his wife Mamie had been in this car just a few hours before.

The Lord surely was on the side of the Allies during the period before, on, and after the date of June 6, 1944. They had to cross one hundred miles of the English Channel to Normandy – Omaha Beach and other planned invasion landing areas. The weather was so bad it was raining sideways, the wind and water so rough the Germans high command figured it would be impossible to launch an invasion. The infamous German, General Rommel, went home to celebrate his wife's birthday. The Lord had other plans, he made the weather bad enough to convince the Germans there would be no invasion. On June 6th He provided a thirty-six hour window, or break in the weather so that General Eisenhower ordered the invasion to begin. There were thousands of allied casualties the first day. If Eisenhower had not taken advantage of that window, the Germans could have wiped out the entire Allied invasion force. (Young people, please, try to learn the truth about your country's history, not what is in today's government – Union written history books.)

Now, back to the weekend with the General's chauffeur and limousine. I do not remember the sarge's name but he said if I would stick with him, he would take care of all expenses. Sounded like a good deal to me, besides, I didn't have anything special planned anyway, but what a weekend it turned out to be. There was not enough action in the small clubs in the rural area around Brunswick, Georgia. So we decided to drive the 85 miles to Jacksonville, Florida. The sarge let me drive the limousine so I would know how everything worked just in case he accidentally had too many drinks. We had dinner and checked the entertainment section in the newspaper. There was a famous big band of that era, Tommy Dorsey, playing in the ballroom of a big hotel and the public was invited to attend the dance. The sarge's eyes lit up, he said, "That's what I've been looking for." We checked into the hotel and he arranged if we got separated I could charge meals in the hotel restaurant to the room. I later learned he had an unlimited expense account. (No credit cards back then.) The admission to the dance was a little less than this sailor was paid for a month. He was right, there were unattached ladies there, dressed in evening gowns or chic little cocktail dresses. He spotted a sharp looking lady with long red hair that he had met somewhere before. He danced with her and brought her to our table. I suddenly felt like just what I was, a still wet behind the ears, eighteen year old who could only legally drink Ginger Ale. I excused myself and told sarge I would see him later. Sunday I decided to take a bus back to Green Cove Air Base to see some of my friends. Monday morning sarge returned to our room, I had not seen him since Saturday night, in just enough time for us to drive back to our duty stations and not be late. When that big limousine pulled into the yacht club, even the officers wanted to know what it was about. Oh, I forgot to mention, sarge found more than what he was looking for.

* * * * *

I was at the yacht club about three months before I was transferred for temporary duty at the air station a few miles down the road. I was assigned to the post office driving a pickup truck. Each day I drove to Brunswick to pick up the mail, help sort, and delivered to various locations on the base. During this time I qualified for my Navy Chauffeurs License. The License and the time working with the mail would soon prove to be a very important turning point of my Navy career. During one of my trips to pick up the mail, I stopped at a drug store with a lunch counter. I noticed a tall, slender, very attractive girl with long, willowy, brunet hair working behind one of the other counters. I said hello to her as I was going out. The next day I went in and she was sitting at the lunch counter, we talked and I asked her for a movie date. During the remainder of the time I was stationed at Saint Simons Island we were together several times a week and went to church on the Sunday's I was off duty. We had some great times and enjoyed being together. She was a sweet and lovely girl, I grew very fond of her, but she was four years older than me and had been married to an alcoholic who abused her. As time went on, I learned she was not the girl for me. There was one weekend, I cannot recall if I was sick or had an injury. I was in Sick Bay (base hospital). We had a Saturday night date. There was only one corpsman on duty. I decided I wanted to keep that date. I put my uniform on, slipped out a side door, making sure the door was unlocked, and took the bus to town. We went to a movie and I was on the last bus going back to the base that night.

    I went back to the side door, "bingo", the door was locked. There was only one other way in. This was a small building with a front porch. I could see the on duty corpsman sitting at his desk. His head was down on his arms. I watched him for a while and decided he was asleep. I took my shoes off, quietly opened the door, held my breath and tip toed across the room, down the hall, and quickly got into my bed. Early the next morning he woke me up for blood pressure and temperature check. He asked me where I was when he made his rounds earlier. I told him I had been to the head (bathroom) several times (which I had). He looked puzzled but muttered something about being "full of crap." I've laughed about it many times, wondering what would have happened if he had woke up while I was tip toeing across that floor with my uniform on and shoes in my hand!! Just another tuff day for a poor ole sailor.

* * * * *

"The war raged on" – Since I was on temporary assignment at this base, I had to take my turn at standing guard duty. Meaning four hours of guarding a particular area twenty-four hours a day. This was wartime and this was a war training base right on the Atlantic Ocean. Enemy sabotage was not only possible but was happening along the coast. German submarines were known to be operating so close, laying mines in the Hampton Roads Shipping Channel at night, their crews could hear people talking and horns blowing on the beaches.

This particular night, my guard duty started at 2400 o'clock (midnight) until 0400 (4 AM). The weather was very cold outside, I was lucky to be guarding inside an airplane hangar. When you relieve the man on duty ahead of you, he hands you a holstered 45 caliber pistol, you check the firearm to make sure it is in firing condition. Guard duty in the middle of the night is very boring, the hours pass slowly. I had learned to break down firearms and put them back together. The pistol I received this time was different from any I had seen before. There were tools handy on a mechanic's table and I decided to look inside this gun, only took a few minutes. Well, the next morning those of us who were on duty that night were ordered to a very disturbed gunnery officer's office. He picked the gun up and wanted to know, "Who in the hell had removed the firing pin?" Well, I know what the firing pin is, where it is, and what it does and I did not go that far but as mad as that Lieutenant was, I was not about to try to explain anything to him. Since no one admitted anything, he gritted his teeth, begged our pardon, wished us a great day and told us where to go, (Oops). I have wondered, since this gun was different, could I have missed something. Oh well, alls well that ends well.

* * * * *

During the months of the second half of 1945, Katherine continued farm work. This was a time when neighbors helped and hired other neighbors to work for them. Tobacco was the main cash crop. Children and their children who moved away would return for the summer to earn money. Katherine was known to be dependable, experienced and a hard worker. She could choose to work for those who paid the most and cooked the "best meals" for their hired hands.

"The War raged on," a constant reminder that people were changing, the world was changing, more and more young people were looking beyond the comfortable and sheltered cocoon in which their parents were raised. This included Katherine, having lost her father, her high school sweetheart and having four brothers serving in the military during a barbaric shooting war. This left Katherine and her mother to run the farm and take care of the two youngest children. Her tremendous work ethics, sense of responsibility and not afraid of hard work, she and her mother were left to shoulder the task of operating the farm. The work was more than they could handle. They leased their tobacco allotment to another farmer. This took the heavy work load off and they were able to maintain a good portion of their income. Her younger brother was now taking over more of the work.

Like most teenagers of that time, Katherine had to grow up fast. She was now a lovely, well developed young woman, not wanting to be a farm wife all of her life. She was dreaming and looking beyond the confines of the life of a farm girl. She was a young woman with a natural curiosity to explore and experience whatever lay beyond the bounds of the close, protected society she had grown up in. The examples of proper conduct and moral values taught to her by a loving, Christian mother and father would serve her well in the decisions she alone would have to make in the unknown world she was soon to venture into.

Early in 1946, Katherine began thinking about nearby, larger towns to find work and be on her own for the first time. She learned that one of her high school friends was going to Rocky Mt., North Carolina to attend a school of nursing. Katherine had relatives there that she could stay with. This seemed to be just what she was looking for, not too close, not too far. She bid a tearful goodbye to her mother and family and was soon on her way to explore a world she had never known. A new life, filled with excitement, new friends, a new job, responsibility, adventure and perhaps meeting that Prince Charming all young girls dream about. (She would meet me later.)

After she settled in with a cousin and her husband in a small but quaint cottage, typical of that era, and within walking distance of the business area. This was the first house she lived in that had an inside bathroom. Right away she set out to find a paying job. With her eagerness, polite manner and being so nice to look at, she soon found her first job, not farm related, in a drug store tending a busy ice cream and soda fountain. This was new and different and she enjoyed it. Now she had a safe, family place to live, a job she liked, and a paycheck. Time to start enjoying her new life by going shopping. You can take the girl out of the country but you can't take the country out of the girl. Even though she had the money, Katherine still liked to buy material and make her own dresses using her aunt's sewing machine, earning her own money, and enjoying a freedom she had never known before. All of this did not betray the work ethics she learned since she was a child, she pitched right in washing dishes, clothes, cleaning the house, helped with the cooking etc., just like today, the bed is always made soon after we get up.

After a few weeks at her new work place, she woke up to a bright, crisp, early spring morning and was enjoying her walk to the drug store, not realizing she was soon to experience her very first romantic encounter in her new world. It would happen suddenly and unexpectedly. She went to the back of the store to put on a special uniform she wore in the soda shop. Suddenly and unexpectedly, (see) she found herself in the arms of a man who was kissing her right smack dab on the lips. She was so dazed and surprised she didn't realize who the elderly man was until he went into the pharmacy and started filling prescriptions. She went to the bathroom, washed, and put on fresh lipstick and made sure he understood he had better not do that ever again. This at least made her day a bit different and gave her something to talk about. Poor fellow, he just couldn't resist the innocent, ravishing beauty that appeared before him. Probably the last exciting moment in his life. I'll bet that's where the term, "dirty old man" originated.

The first guy to invite Katherine to dinner and maybe a movie was also a bit older. She went with him two times before deciding she really did not care for him. A real coincidence, her friend, the nurse, later married this man. Just as nature intended, wherever there is honey, the bees will always find it. One day a young marine came to the soda fountain and found something far sweeter than the ice cream he wanted. It is understood, marines are an extended part of the Navy. Sailors have been in existence for thousands of years. Sailors and marines have built-in antennas. Whenever a pretty girl is near, our antennas go up and lead us straight to them. He asked her for a date. This developed to the point where he went with her on the bus one weekend when she was going home. While there, he asked Mother Jackson for permission to marry her daughter. Katherine doesn't know what her mom's answer was but his home was in Wisconsin and he was Jewish. His mother objected to him marrying a Christian girl and Katherine did not want to live that far away from her own family. (Thank you Lord!) His marine duties allowed him to come to Rocky Mount every other weekend. She never saw him again. In the meantime, as often happens when relatives try to live together, Katherine had a misunderstanding with her cousin's husband so she quit her job, packed up and returned home.

* * * * *

Needless to say, Mother Jackson was very happy to have her daughter back again and Katherine quickly resumed her chores. She was there about two months when a high school girlfriend heard that she was back and came to see her to catch up on the latest about each other. This friend was now living and working as a telephone operator in Norfolk, Virginia. She suggested maybe Katherine could do the same thing and go to work as an operator. She asked her to go back with her and they could stay together until she found a job. This decision would be the next step on the road to meeting the man she would marry.

"The cold war raged on." Katherine was excited, they would be returning to Norfolk the very next day and would be riding with a neighbor friend. She was all packed and ready to go. When they arrived Katherine's day got off to a great start. When she saw the friend she would be riding with she nearly flipped. He was a ranking naval officer, a Commander. Those white summer uniforms with the three wide, gold stripes on the epaulette on each shoulder and the gold scrambled eggs on the cap really impress the ladies, especially those right off the farm and not used to seeing them. She was quite taken with him. She had never seen a man like this, her knight in shining armor. She thought he was the handsomest man she had ever seen. (She hadn't seen me yet – yuk – yuk)

Katherine was again off to unknown exciting adventures that would change her life forever. The inborn values she had been taught all of her life by her parents, family, church, friends, and even her non-union, non-government run schools taught the social graces, and young ladies how to be proper young ladies. During those days in the past, self promoting, profit hungry union bosses did not own and rule the schools like today. Pulling the strings of many puppet school leaders and politicians in their rule or ruin goals of those in their ivory towers. The education of students is only a by-product that must be tolerated in their quest for power. The schools then were run by "local yokuls" who were actually dumb enough to think there was a difference between boys and girls. Boys were taught useless hobbies like engine repair, woodworking, farming, engineering, etc, even how to be "proper gentlemen" and good husbands, fathers, and providers for their families. What a waste of time and talent. Boys and girls were not even taught to "Just Say No" because they didn't know what to say no to. Just imagine, those virtuous, poorly educated teachers didn't even bother to teach the girls important subjects like "how to put a condom on a cucumber." Much less, what the word condom even meant and teenage pregnancy was all the way down to three or four percent. Shucks, if they had been properly educated, like they are today, and tried a little harder (no pun intended), they could have had a much higher score, maybe even 40-60% pregnancy (like today). All of this, over time, would be taxed to the limit by the world Katherine was entering. But right now she was excited.

* * * * *

As they neared the Portsmouth – Norfolk city limit, Katherine's eyes were wide open, seeing sights she had never seen. She had her first ferry ride from Portsmouth to Norfolk. Wondered why there were railroad tracks in the middle of the street in downtown Norfolk until she spotted her first trolley car, which she would be riding many times. She had never been in a city this size and was fascinated by so many tall buildings. They continued through Norfolk to Ocean View, where her friend lived, and saw the Atlantic Ocean for the first time. She said goodbye to her handsome Commander, thanked him for the ride and he went back to the war. His family lived near Pinetown and they all attended the same church. She had seen him before.

They very next morning they walked to the trolley car stop; she was excited about her first ride. She stepped in, dropped her nickel in the coin box and away they went into downtown Norfolk to the telephone company to apply for her new job. They were not hiring at that time but took her application and promised a call in the near future. She needed an income right away. Her friend had already started her workday. Again, Katherine needed no one to hold her hand. She walked to the nearby downtown area and just as she had in Rocky Mount, she set out to find her own job, but this time she had a base of experience to work from. She went to one of the largest drug chains at that time, they were not hiring. Next, a store of a smaller chain on Granby Street, Whelan Drug, they had a nice lunch counter and a few tables in back. Early the next morning she rode the trolley into Norfolk by herself and reported for her first day of work as a waitress in this neat little drug store restaurant, serving mostly downtown business people, shoppers, and of course service men.

"The cold war raged on." The Lord now had Katherine in place for our eventual meeting but it was not to be for more than a year. In all His wisdom, He knew neither of us was mature enough or ready for the lifelong union He was preparing for us. She was a good dependable worker, she made friends easily and as time went on, she was promoted to other departments in the store.

When the telephone company called with an operator's position open, she turned them down, she liked her job at the store and her new friends. This decision was more important than she could possibly imagine. She had to be in that store for us to meet. Now it was time to find her own place to live closer to work. Her friends suggested the Y.W.C.A. She had never heard of a Y.W.C.A. (Young Women's Christian Association). They did not have one in any of the small towns she had lived in. The one in Norfolk was only six blocks from the store. This was the ideal place for a young woman like her. Close to work and all downtown Norfolk, a nice cafeteria for meals, churches, and a park with a lake nearby. The building had three floors and no elevator, younger women, like Katherine, were assigned to the walk up third floor. Two girls shared a room. She saw and experienced her first shower bath. This was to be her home away from home for the next eighteen months.

She soon settled into a daily living and work routine and making many new friends at the "Y" and at work. Since most of the girls on the third floor were working and away from home, near the same age, and sharing many of the same interest, they would often gather in each other's rooms for an evening of girl talk, birthday parties, or any other special occasions was a reason to bring in snacks, soft drinks, etc. For the most part, they didn't need anything special to have a yak-yak party.

* * * * *

The Y.W.C.A. was located in a neighborhood which, in the recent past, was the elite, upper class section of Norfolk with large, beautiful homes; some now were business or apartment buildings. In the very next block from the Y.W.C.A., the U.S.O. (United Service Organization) had leased a large home to welcome and offer the service men and women a place to relax, play games, great snacks, and always plenty of coffee and doughnuts. In the evening, young women would come in to dance with the guys in the ballroom to juke box music. Everything was discretely supervised, no alcoholic beverages, if a guy came in with alcohol on his breath, he was quietly asked to leave. A girl could dance with the same service man all evening only if she came in with him as a date and they just wanted a nice safe place to spend the evening. Many of the girls at the "Y" were regulars at the USO club. Volunteering to prepare sandwiches and other snacks and on special occasions they would get all dressed up, make themselves beautiful, go to the USO club and help decorate for the occasion, dance with the guys and just like Cinderella, all return to the "Y" before the midnight curfew.

One Saturday night the other girls asked Katherine to go with them. She dressed special, went to the club, and sat down to watch. Soon a young sailor came to the table and asked Katherine to dance with him. She was nervous. She had to tell him her father did not allow her to go to dances; this was her first and she didn't know how to dance. This probably delighted him to no end, actually finding a girl like this. He begged her to let him teach her a few dance steps.

Now, for her first time she was actually dancing with a guy, she had a good time at the party and became a regular at the USO club. This was good wholesome fun for a young woman just starting a new life for herself. Her new world had grown a little wider, but for the most part her time was spent with her work, with her friends at the "Y", occasional movie dates or eating at a different restaurant, and attending church or going to the park with friends. As often as possible when she had a long weekend off, she would return home to visit with her mother and family, she just was not one of those who drifted into being a sophisticated, big city girl who would put on airs when she returned to the farm. When she walked thru the door of her home and greeted her mother and family, she went right to work. She carried buckets of water to a large, iron kettle in the yard just outside the kitchen door and built a fire under the kettle to heat water to put into the old hand wringing washing machine. Remember, no electricity, so she started the gasoline engine to wash the clothes. This was modern, before that she put the clothes into the big iron kettle and used a hard scrub board and homemade soap to wash the clothes. Then, they had to be hung out to dry and ironed using heavy irons heated on the wood burning kitchen stove.

* * * * *

As I wrote before, where there is honey, you will find the bees. Whelan Drug Store was located on a busy corner in downtown Norfolk, Virginia. The same young sailor who taught Katherine her first dance steps at the USO came into the store and ask her for a date. (Now I wonder how he knew where she worked?) He was her first date in Norfolk. She arranged a double date with her roommate and now she went to her first private night club for an evening of dancing. During the week, the girls at the Y.W.C.A. had to be in by midnight. Her new world continued to expand.

In Norfolk she was as far away from home as she had ever been. Also working in the store was a young married couple who had become close friends with Katherine. Sometimes when they worked the same hours they would either give her a ride to the "Y" or invite her to their home for games, etc. There was another young man who was a department manager in the store. His home was in Newark, New Jersey, just across the Hudson River from New York City. He was planning a trip up to his home and he invited the young couple and Katherine to go with him. She had never dated him, they were all just good friends and they decided it would be a fun trip. They packed their bags and Katherine was now off to an even more exciting adventure to see really big cities with skyscraper buildings that went right up into the clouds. Katherine saw her first drive in restaurant where girls on roller skates came to your car, took your order, and returned with a tray full of food and drinks. The tray fit nicely over the door and everyone could enjoy their food without leaving the car. They enjoyed the short visit with his family, the girls shared a room and the guys had a room.

Her new world grew even wider and there were more adventures yet to come. Yes, I knew Katherine had a life before I came into the picture, she was a very attractive young woman and of course she had dates, but I cannot find the words to describe how it pleases me to know that no serious relationships developed during the year she was in Norfolk before I met her.

* * * * *

Many things happened at each of my assigned bases but I am only writing about the more interesting things as I remember them.

Soon after the invasion of Europe, thousands of German prisoners were being shipped to the United States and dispersed to all military bases. This brought us face to face with the enemy we had been taught to hate and trained to kill. About ten percent were still considered dangerous and were put under lock and key. The other ninety percent were put to work on all types of jobs such as, clearing and draining swampland in our part of the country. As time went on, according to their skills, they became trustees and given lower end jobs such as janitorial, grounds keepers. Many were highly skilled machinists, mechanics, metal smiths, etc. This gave us a chance to know our enemies on a personal basis. Most of them were just like us. They wanted to go home and be with their families and start their lives all over again. They laughed, they joked, we shared pictures of our families, wives, children, girlfriends, etc. We taught each other a few words of our languages. They were just as shocked and disgusted as we were when we learned about the terrible death camps and atrocities committed in their country. I was amazed at the skill of several of the ones I came into contact with. They could take a spoon, knife or a scrap piece of metal and turn it into a beautiful piece of jewelry, bracelet, necklace, ring, belt buckle, etc. They made me several pieces, I don't know what happened to them but I sure wish I had them now, with that history they would be very valuable today.

* * * * *

"The war raged on," April 12, 1945, the news came in, our wartime leader had died. It was as though a terrible shock wave had come over our entire nation. President Franklin D. Roosevelt, the only three term president. Americans were truly united behind one strong leader, galvanized into action. Too busy defending our country to bother with an election. Not so today, 2006, the selfish, old Neanderthal career politicians and every little radical group are forcing our president to fight a war within, and a war without, and our enemies are invading our country without a shot being fired while we bicker among ourselves. For the first time in my life, I fear for my country. We are not united and our committed enemies sense our weakness. But I have faith that the basic core of real Americans will rise up, throw out the bums and that God will provide a leader in the caliber of Roosevelt, "Give 'em hell – Harry Truman," Ronald Reagan and no, not pretty boy, Prince of Camelot, John F. Kennedy who at the last minute abandoned our allies at the "Bay of Pigs" Cuba, our only chance to take out the communist Cuban dictator, Fidel Castro. They were left to be slaughtered or imprisoned by Castro.

* * * * *

Time again to move on, I bid farewell to St. Simons Island, Georgia, packed my sea bag and off to the Naval Base, Norfolk, Virginia, for a short stay. I had not yet earned my crow and first stripe, still a seaman first class, next to the lowest of the lowest. I was about to get my comeuppance, meaning I should have been a petty officer by now. For the first time I was assigned K.P. duty, meaning kitchen police, meaning if a garbage can lets itself get filled up, it was my duty to grab him, wrestle him to a dumping station and disgorge everything inside, water hose him out, and return him to a respectable position with the other cans. Anyway, I didn't mind it for the short time I was there because I soon learned my next assignment was what I had been begging and waiting for since I first joined the Navy. "Happy day," my orders came in and my dream was finally going to come true. I was the only one in my original group to be assigned as a crewman aboard a ship.

At this time there were no underwater tunnels or miles long bridges out of Norfolk. I took the three hour long ferry ride to a point in Maryland where I boarded a Pullman Train to Portland, Maine. Pullman coach equals seats converted into upper and lower sleeping bunks at night. It took two days and two nights for the crowded train, with a five hour layover at Grand Central Station in New York City, to reach Portland, Maine. We arrived early in the morning. There was a station wagon waiting to take me to Fleet Landing where I boarded a launch taking Navy personnel to the islands and ships anchored in Casco Bay, a quiet inlet for ships operating in the North Atlantic. I asked the coxswain operating the boat to point out my first ship – The U.S.S. Harold J. Ellison – DD 864, so I could see her from a distance for my first time. I couldn't believe how excited and nervous I was, there were lobster pot floating markers (like plastic milk cartons, but no plastic then) all over the bay. Soon I heard, "Hey sailor, there she is, your new ship, The 'Ellison' dead ahead." I guess my eyes were bulging, a beautiful, graceful, sleek fighting ship, lying serenely at anchor in mirror smooth water. This was to be my home for the next two years.

Soon, we pulled alongside, I stepped onto the boarding platform, and just like you see in the movies, I wanted to make a good first impression. I was wearing my dress blue uniform, white hat, squared on my forehead, my sea bag on my left shoulder, mustered up as much stiff military posture as I could, and walked up the ladder to the landing before boarding the ship. I smartly saluted the ensign (flag) turned to salute the officer of the deck and announced, "Seaman first class Wally Hillman, requesting permission to come aboard, <u>Sir</u>." I missed the first step going down, my sea bag made it onboard the ship before I did, I ended up on my knees looking for my white hat, my hair down in my eyes. The officer turned the other way and when we both regained some of our composure all he could say was, we've been expecting you Hillman, go aft to the crews quarters and someone will show you your bunk. I heard about this for months but one positive came out of it, most everybody on the ship knew my name because of my grand entrance coming aboard. What they didn't know was that soon I would know the name of every crewman and officer on the ship and many of them would envy my position.

In the after crews quarters, I'm not exactly sure, about 200 men, possibly more in the different sections. Three bunks high, I got a top bunk because I only weighed 135 pounds. I had to step up on each of the bunks below me and my stomach was not up in the electric cables, air conditioning and heating ducts just over me. The ship's twin screws (propellers) were below and about fifteen feet further aft from us. When the ship was under way and at sea, those screws were turning twenty-four hours a day. It's like living near a railroad track, after a while you don't even hear the trains going by. When you do not hear those screws turning, especially when you are in high seas, you could be in bad trouble. No control, you are at the mercy of the sea. The hum of those engines lulled you to sleep.

* * * * *

While I was working at the Newport News ship yards, I had a chance to go aboard a destroyer. The aircraft carriers I helped build were so massive you would need a very complicated map to find your way to every compartment and passage way and even more strict regulations than a large naval base. There were thousands of personnel on board. I just did not want to serve on a carrier. The destroyers were just the opposite, 325 officers and crewmen. Like living in a large city or a small town where everyone knows each other. More firepower per square foot than a battleship, able to attack or defend herself against anything from the air, surface, or below the water surface. Built for speed to take care of trouble, find trouble, cause trouble, or look for trouble before trouble got away. They were called the expendable ships. One of the first lines of defense, especially for a convoy of ships. A lean, mean, fighting machine. We were constantly drilling until we didn't have to think, our actions were automatic. Last in line, behind the fleet, destroyer captains have been known to sacrifice their ship of only 325 men, including himself, to purposely engage a larger and faster pursuing fleet of enemy ships by unexpectedly turning into their path and firing all his torpedoes, every gun blasting away, knowing the enemy fleet would be forced to slow down long enough to deal with and blow this little flea out of the water. This actually happened in the Pacific and other areas. The single little destroyer's torpedoes sunk two large Japanese warships and damaged others before going down. Their guns were still firing while the ship was sinking. The entire Japanese fleet was forced to deal with one destroyer long enough for the smaller and slower American fleet, heavily loaded with ammunitions, men, and equipment for invading enemy islands, to escape.

Today the liberal news media and turncoat politicians, "you self serving cowardly bastards," would gleefully add 325 to their daily or hourly tally of military deaths, not even mentioning the 325 lives that were bravely sacrificed to save the lives of thousands of young fighting men.

* * * * *

Destroyers have a nick-name, "tin cans". In order to be fast and maneuverable, you have to lose weight. Battleships, for example, have very thick main deck armor plates to withstand 500 pound bombs dropped by airplanes. Tin cans had no armor, just about one inch main deck plates. They were like corks in high seas we were either cresting the waves or way down in the trough.

"The war raged on." D-Day, June 6, 1944, the invasion of Europe begins. The Germans had been preparing for this event many years. Camouflaged defensive weapons of all types were hidden all along the coasts. A shipmate of mine had served aboard the "Destroyer Laffey DD724" during the first part of the invasion. He said the Destroyers could operate in shallow waters so close to the beach, when the Germans fired their guns the Destroyer crews could see the smoke and blow their bunkers right out of the cliffs. The Battleships, Cruisers, etc were so far out in deeper water they could not see the targets. The Allied invasion troops were being cut down by the hundreds by the hidden enemy. Destroyers turned the tide of battle in many areas, from defeat and many more men dying, to a very important victory.

* * * * *

The closest I came to actual combat was during one of our earliest trips to the far North Atlantic. I had been on duty several hours at my sea station in the C.I.C. room watching the radar scope. I had just stepped outside onto the upper deck just below the bridge for fresh air and rest my eyes, when a "lookout" screamed the alarm, "Torpedo – 10 o'clock deep," exactly below where I was standing. Just seconds before impact, I actually saw that torpedo, no time or place to run. It passed under our ship, evidently meant for a larger, deeper draft vessel. No other ship was hit and its origin never found, or disclosed to the crew. We rescued a number of pilots who had to ditch their planes in the cold ocean water. I was either lucky or my "Guardian Angel" was watching over me again.

* * * * *

Now, back to Portland, Maine, where I first saw and went aboard my ship. I can't remember what my first duty assignment was but it did not last very long. When we were not on work duty a favorite gathering place was on the main deck, fantail, stern or after part of the ship, all the same place, where we could relax, sit and talk. I learned here that the mailman would soon be transferred off the ship. I worked in the mailroom for a short time when I was stationed at the air base, St. Simons Island, Georgia. Mostly driving a truck picking up the mail. I decided I wanted his job, I went to the communications officer, part of his division was the mail. I told him I had experience in the post office and wanted to be the ship's mailman. I'm glad he didn't ask how much experience. I really knew next to nothing but I knew I could learn some from the current mailman and from others on the nearby tin cans in our squadron. Also, when he checked my records and found I held a Navy chauffer drivers license, I got the job without any more questions.

There were some disappointed guys who had been on the ship for a good while who wanted the job. I am a firm believer, "It's the squeaky wheel that gets the grease." The first mouse to the trap gets all the cheese. 'Oops, better rethink that one. I went right to the decision maker and convinced him, "I was da man." There were only two one-man offices on the entire ship. I now had mine and I let the captain have the other one. The post office was in a neat little compartment just aft of the after crews quarters, portside. The goodies kept coming. In the Navy you have two jobs, the one you get paid to do, the other is your duty station while at sea and/or General Quarters under combat conditions. I was assigned as radar operator in the C.I.C. room (Combat Information Center) a nice, warm, inside, sit down job operating the extended eyes of the ship. In direct contact with the bridge, transmitted communication comes through the C.I.C. room. I was now a bit more comfortable with the day to day routine of living aboard a Navy warship.

* * * * *

You had to learn a new language. I am going to name only a few. To you ole "salty dawgs", if I get something wrong, don't forget it's been sixty years. You are no longer standing on a floor surrounded by walls and a ceiling, you are standing on a deck surrounded by bulkheads and an overhead. You do not go left-right-front-back, it's port-starboard-forward (bow)-aft (stern), you do not go up-down, you go topside-below, bathroom equals head, kitchen equals galley, dining room equals mess hall, food equals chow, a few officers $#@*%! -- Oops, sorry officers, most of you were regular guys, but I guess when you must exercise authority you will step on some toes.

I had two weeks to learn all I could before the mailman was transferred. Now I am officially the ships mailman. Those who had not learned my name called me stamps. The ships mail room had a safe. First official duty, the communications officer came in to change the combination on the safe. He instructed me to dial in my own numbers to open the safe. I had my own combination lock on my personal locker so I used the same numbers on the mail room safe because I had them memorized. That same lock is now on the door of a little red utility barn my family and I built. Each day the ship's "plan of the day on the bulletin board, listing each hour, the more important things to be done, my name will be there every day, 0900 Hillman, mail trip motor launch." On the ship's intercom I will hear the Bos'n Pipe signal and, "Now hear this, now hear this, Hillman, U.S. mailman report to the quarter deck for mail run." I would join in the motor launch the mailmen from the three other destroyers that sailed with us in our squadron, the "USS Charles R. Ware DD 865", "USS Kenneth D. Bailey DD 713", and the "USS Ernest G. Small DD 838", the ship I served on after I left the "USS Harold J. Ellison DD 864". We were usually in an open, "motor whale boat". If the weather was warm we talked, enjoyed watching the sea otters floating on their backs, eating their food. The lobstermen taking in their traps. Different scenes depending on the port we were in. When the scenery wasn't much, we did what all mailmen are accused of doing, reading the post cards, but I liked the unsealed love letters best, especially the ones with all the "xxx-ooo-swak-ily's etc."

Once in the dead of winter, when we were anchored off Argencia, Newfoundland, the mail trip going into port, we were moving into the wind and were covered with ice when we arrived at the landing. On the return trip the wind was blowing to our backs, my ship was first. None of us realized that sprays of water was being blown into our pockets and our gloved hands were frozen to our pockets. My hands were so cold I could not grip the ladder up the side of our ship. Shipmates had to climb down and hoist me up the ladder. I went to sick bay, was given a shot of something, my hands were put into, I believe, cold water and warmed up until feeling came back, then the stinging started, anyway, to this day my hands stay cold and sting during the winter.

* * * * *

While my ship was operating out of "Casco Bay" at Portland, Maine (I really like this port) I experienced my first and only brig time (navy jail). I was innocent, innocent I tell you, "somebody else did it," lemme outta here!! Oops, got a little carried away there. I was in town a little early, I decided to take in a movie and meet with some of my shipmates later. After the movie, I came out of the theater, it was raining a little and I was walking down the street putting my raincoat on when a "shore patrol" wagon stopped beside me. One of them got out, carrying a "billy club". He asked for my liberty card, when I handed it to him, he ordered me into the patrol wagon. When I asked him, "What was the problem?" he said my raincoat was not buttoned up and I was out of uniform. He had my liberty card and I could see he was not going to listen to reason, so I was locked in the wagon with two other sailors who happened to be my shipmates. They too had been picked up for no good reason. We were taken to fleet landing, charges were written up and we spent the night in the pokey, slammer, crowbar hotel, brig, whatever.

Early the next morning we were sprung, hardened criminals, we were escorted to the first liberty boat going to our ship. We also learned the shore patrol guy had been punished and given extra duty, he took his spite out on us and others by trying to fill the brig and giving his chief more work to do. Two hours later, while I was making the mail run with the other ships mailmen, I told them what had happened and about spending the night in the brig. One of the older mailmen said, "Don't worry about it, I'll show you what to do." When we picked up our mail from the fleet post office, he looked through my mail and took out a brown, US Navy envelope. It was not sealed and did not have a U.S. Postage stamp, so no postal laws were broken. He removed three reports of minor offences, including mine, tore them up, put them back into the envelope along with a metal bolt and sent them to the bottom of the bay. There were no other records of minor offenses and now I know what to do with them each day. Reports more than minor had to go to the ships office.

* * * * *

Every warships mailman was required to wear a holstered, 45 automatic pistol when carrying mail. Other precautions were taken when we were sent to pick up what the Navy called "Guard Mail". These were special messages to the squadron or individual ship. Each mailman was taken by motor launch to a particular island station or building, when operating within a naval military base, to receive the Guard Mail and deliver it directly to an officer aboard his ship. No side business was permitted. However, mother nature sometimes interferes with the best made "plans of mice or men." It was an absolutely calm, beautiful summer day on "Casco bay", the water was mirror smooth. The motor launch came alongside to pick me up for a Guard Mail run to a nearby island station. We were cruising along, enjoying watching the cute, little sea otters floating on their backs eating their food. The big fish below, swirling the water. I was relaxed, sitting near the back of the open boat talking with the two man crew. So calm and peaceful, suddenly, without warning, a loud crunch, the bow went high out of the water, the boat turned on its side as it came down throwing the coxswain, standing up, steering the boat, into the water. Luckily, the boat righted itself without taking on water. We fished the "man overboard" out of the water, tried to calm our nerves, started the engine and were on our way. We had hit the top of a large, unmarked, just below the surface rock, I don't know how much damage was done to the boat, but that was enough excitement for one day.

* * * * *

While in Casco Bay, we had a new captain come aboard, he was a heavy set, red haired, red faced Irishman, very loud and boisterous after a night of sipping a wee bit too much Irish dew. One of those nights while aboard the motor launch returning to his ship, he was looking at the dozens of lobster trap markers floating in the water. He bellowed out so loudly it could be heard all across the bay that he wanted "a fresh lobster for every man on my ship." Evidently, he was heard by the right people because early in the morning 325 lobsters, just out of the water, were delivered to our ship. What a surprise for the mess cooks, having to change a meal menu for 325 men at the last minute. Fast forward, evening meal, most of the crew were like me, never even seen a lobster. Now we were looking at a big red creature that was looking back at us, tail over one side of our tray and claws over the other side and we were supposed to eat that thing? There were a few guys who knew what to do. Soon we were all pulling, cracking, dipping into melted butter and yes, the rich food caused some loose bowels. Now, when I occasionally have lobster, my thoughts drift back to those moments in my life sixty-five years ago.

* * * * *

When we finally kicked the German's butts and Hitler and his sweetie pie, Eva Braun, committed suicide – the Italian people shot and hung the hog joweled Italian dictator, Benito Mussolini and his sweetie pie's naked butts upside down like hogs in a market place. Truman exploded the second atomic bomb over Nagasaki, convincing the Japanese that we were fed up with the war <u>they</u> <u>started</u>. For you bleeding hearts who were not even born then, who have been brain washed by brain washed college professors who also were not even a sparkle in their father's eye, Hiroshima and Nagasaki both had military bases and war industries. The Japanese government made them legitimate war targets. The civilian population was <u>showered</u> <u>with</u> <u>thousands</u> <u>of</u> <u>leaflets</u> <u>warning</u> them to leave. They had a chance. Hundreds of thousands of Americans had been killed or wounded and no leaflets were dropped. I wonder how many tears you have shed for your own countrymen who did not start the war but had to die so you would not have to be speaking Japanese or

German right now. If the Japanese homeland had been invaded, easily a million people would have died.

Anyway, the world was now enjoying an uneasy peace. On special holidays, cities along the coast were allowed to invite Navy warships to tie up or anchor nearby. The townspeople were invited to come aboard, visit and be given a guided tour of the ship. In return the city would provide some special entertainment for the ship's crew. Plenty of food was always provided. Some cities had big popular stage shows. Somehow we seemed to cotton to the big bands and dances. All we had to do was shower, shampoo, shave, shine, show up and a room full of beauties was waiting just for us. This broke our hearts, here we were, all shy and innocent as babes in arms, wondering what we were supposed to do with all these girls. Somehow nature has a way of taking its course. The girls knew they were as safe as they wanted to be because when that last liberty boat pulls out, if you are not on board you had better prepare for a long swim or hope the girl you just couldn't say goodbye to fast enough has a boat tied up somewhere and is willing to row herself back from dumping you off at your ship. Was it worth it? Well, that just depends on what really made you miss that last liberty boat. The Navy has a nasty way of showing its displeasure when a crewman misses his ships departure.

* * * * *

My ship was operating out of "Casco Bay", Portland, Maine. I don't remember the holiday, it was during perfect warm weather and the ocean was calm. We had a delightful sail to a place I had never heard of,

North of Portland, in the "Nova Scotia" area. We left the open waters of the Atlantic Ocean behind and were soon entering the "Frenchman Bay" area. We began seeing small, perfectly round, tree covered islands, there were no flat, sandy, desolate beaches as I remember. The shoreline was high, tree covered, and lined with large, million dollar mansions. This was one of my favorite, most beautiful places we visited. This was Bar Harbor, Maine, home to families like the Campbell's of the Campbell Soup Company. The water was deep enough for us to sail right into a serene cove. We dropped anchor a few hundred feet out from the village's small boat docking which led up a hill to the town area. You would expect to find yachts and other large boats, they no doubt were nearby, but this cove was clean and really pretty. The lifeboat motor launch was lowered and guess who was among the first to go ashore? Two officers and the mailman of course, sometimes I think even the captain was a little envious of my job. Townspeople were around the shore and on the dock. I was in dress blue uniform, packing a 45 caliber pistol on my side which was required of all mailmen. As we climbed out of the boat, people began to clap and yell, "Welcome to Bar Harbor." I felt like a celebrity or hero or something. To those of us who served on the ship, this was just routine. Most of these people had never seen an actual warship up close and real. Guns of every size and type bristling from stem to stern. Every piece of then, modern technology, to find and destroy the enemy and this ship had done just that.

  As we walked along the walkway, people were shaking our hands, thanking us for coming and for what we did during the war. One older gentleman, his wife, children, and grandchildren got our attention and they all hugged each of us. The officers walked on. He told me they had lost their youngest son, a sailor, in the war. I looked down at two little children, their arms around my legs, looking up at me with big wide eyes. I saw the tears in their grandmother's eyes. I asked if these were his children. No, he was not married, these were his sister's children. My heart went out to this close, wonderful family. This gave me another chance to see the other side of war. They wrote their phone number on a piece of paper and invited me to their home for dinner. By this time the motor launch was arriving with other officers, they were receiving the same treatment. I approached a group of nurses and nuns with their hands out to shake our hands and hug us. One of the nurses remarked it was awesome when the ship suddenly appeared around the trees and headed into the cove. It made chills run down my spine (I don't know how she knew I was on board.) The nuns said it was exciting and frightening, I've always wondered if she meant the ship or the sailors. Others remarked they wanted their children to see something they would never forget. This was the largest ship ever to enter this cove and the first real warship. Actually, a destroyer is one of the smaller warships but it looked large in this cove. I was sure proud of her, sitting in such beautiful surroundings and people taking her picture. The folks were really nice. I asked for directions to the post office and went on with my business.

* * * * *

A good friend of mine at Green Cove Springs Airbase in Florida lived in a nearby town, about forty miles inland from Bar Harbor, Bangor, Maine. I called him from the post office, he was excited to hear from me. He would not take no for an answer when he insisted on driving over to pick me up and return for dinner and meeting the girl he had told me about everyday for six months. They were married and had a new baby girl. They also owned a nice restaurant he wanted me to see and he would cook a special meal. He would pick me up at 5 PM the next day. That same day was visitor's day on the ship, with a big dance that night.

Now the fun begins, I had missed chow time on the ship and the P.O. guys suggested a neat little restaurant nearby. I will tell you now, for some reason I have always been attracted to blondes. On the way to the restaurant I passed the village beauty shop. Sitting in the window was a very pretty, blonde beautician, giving her customer a manicure. (On my honor, the following really did happen.) Our eyes met and she winked at me. Being a proper gentleman, I continued on, walking backwards, but I just had to know if she actually winked or had something in her eye. So I walked back and watched her out of the corner of my eye. She gave me a nice smile. I knew she could not talk right then and I needed to find that restaurant so I had to walk by again, this time she laughed.

In a village like this, restaurants were limited and you were not given a private table, you sat in the next available chair. I was next in line when a couple got up. I was given one of the two places with an empty chair beside me. I was served my meal. The other folks at the table were asking me so many questions I could hardly eat my food. (Now this honestly did happen!) The blonde beautician came in and was given the chair next to me. Hallelujah!!! Little Bible lingo there. We talked and I invited her to visit the ship the next day, I would give her a private tour. I learned she owned the beauty shop and had to go back to work. I took care of the mail and during the night a terrible thought hit me. I was so excited about meeting her I completely forgot I would not be going to the dance the next night. I didn't get any more sleep that night, my legs were sore from trying to kick my own butt. "What a revoltin situation this was."

* * * * *

Later, I told one of my buddies about this, he said, "You mean the blonde I saw you showing around the ship?" Yep – he said, "Turn around, I'm gonna kick your butt and I'll make it hurt!" I did – he did – it did. Not really. I enjoyed visiting my friend but when we started back from Bangor, my real problem began. We traveled about two miles when he had engine trouble. It was too late for repairs. I had to take the last bus back to Bar Harbor and it was crowded, stopping every few miles to pick up or let passengers off. I arrived in Bar Harbor too late for the last liberty boat back to the ship. It was only about the length of four football fields from me, but it may as well have been ten miles. It was a real dark night. The boat dock was well lighted, a chill in the damp air and lonesome, lonesome, lonesome. I was miserable sitting there thinking about my nice warm bunk on the ship. As if this weren't enough, I was also in trouble and getting cold. I started walking to the different sections and levels of the dock just to have something to do and keep a little warmer. These Navy uniform pants have no pockets.

In a darkened overhang of the dock I spotted a small fishing boat tied up and it had a single oar lying in the bottom. I shooed away the little devil sitting on my shoulder. The wheels in my brain started turning. Here I am, cold, nothing to do, and hours before daylight, there's a boat with an oar, I'm a sailor, I know how to handle a boat, and out there is my ship with a good warm bunk. I couldn't resist the temptation, I put my white hat under my blue jumper turned my long Navy collar and cuffs under so the white stripes wouldn't show, untied that boat, grabbed the one oar, and got as low as I could get on my knees in the bow so I wouldn't be as easy to see. I started quietly paddling with one oar a zig zag course out to the ship, staying in the shadows of trees as much as possible. It was really dark, I quietly approached the fantail (back) so I could easily crawl up on deck, push the boat as far away as possible and head for my bunk. Suddenly, out of the darkness, I heard my name being called, "Hillman! Hillman!" It shocked me! I thought it was the Lord wanting to have a word with me. Night vision glasses had not yet been invented. The voice went on, "Hillman, the O.D. (officer on duty) said you better take that boat back or you will be charged with stealing a boat." "Another revoltin development." I sat up, disgusted, wondering how they not only could see me in the darkness but they knew who it was. It seemed like a long way back to that dock, paddling with one oar.

I tied the boat just as it was, walked back up the dock, sat down figuring at least three more miserable hours. I guess this was another time my "Guardian Angel" was watching out for me in spite of my actions. In about fifteen minutes I started hearing voices, then footsteps. Two young boys carrying fishing rods and a bait bucket were walking toward me. One of them said, "Hey sailor, you need a ride out to your ship?" I couldn't believe this, but wait til I tell you what happened next. I followed them down to the next level right to the little fishing boat I had just tied up. I had a bit of a guilty conscience flare up but I just couldn't bring myself to tell them what almost happened to their boat.

* * * * *

That warm bunk of mine really felt good and I had four hours of sleep. I was put on report for missing the last liberty boat. Townspeople were there early to watch the ship pull out. I looked closely to see if my little blonde beautician was in the crowd but I guess one of the other guys took care of that. Thanks a lot – what's that old saying about "spilt milk" or "water over the dam"?

We backed slowly out of the cove and Bar Harbor faded into the distance, and locked into my memory forever, but not thought of until over sixty years later. What wonderful and not so wonderful, but interesting memories we all have stored in that fantastic computer God built into each of us to record every thought, action, deed, everything we see, hear, each word we speak. It was all part of another unplanned, interesting adventure.

We were now underway, heading back to sea for a few days of training. After breakfast the Bos'ns

Schrill whistle piped into the ships intercom. "Now hear this – now hear this, the following names report to '01 Deck' for Captains Mast." (The lowest form of Court - Marshal) Punishment for minor offenses, my name was called. I had missed the last liberty boat and was late returning. I was confined to the ship and given extra duty hours. We were at sea during my confinement so I could not leave the ship anyway. My extra duty hours were spent painting the mess hall and were over by the time we returned to port. The Captains Mast was not entered into my record and I kind of like a little painting. There is just one part of all this I wish had turned out different. Guess which part? Yuk yuk yuk.

* * * * *

During January of 1947, we joined the other ships in our squadron for training exercises with submarines out of New London, Connecticut, the Atlantic Fleet Submarine Base. On our voyage south we were to spend one night anchored at Block Island which lies off the coast of Rhode Island. I don't know why we were going to anchor way out there in mostly open waters. The seas were calm with some ground swells. Four destroyers at anchor, except for duty personnel, all crews were sleeping. About 0400 (AM), in the distance we were suddenly awakened by a familiar loud clang, clang, clang on the P.A. speakers – "All hands man your emergency stations – This is not a drill – I repeat, this is not a drill – All hands man your emergency stations." Constant training brought all the crew out of a sound sleep, into their clothes and rushing to their stations. Traffic rules, to avoid collisions of a lot of men on the move, "starboard side, forward and upward – portside, aft and downward. No conversation, just get to your station." Although it was not our ship, many of us were awakened and went to see what the problem was. It was the USS Small. I did not know it at that time but it was the ship I would be transferred to in less than a year, very slowly drifting toward shallow water.

We heard the loud crunching, grinding sound, the Small leaned over to starboard about ten or fifteen degrees – and remained in the starboard list about 400 yards off Block Island, hard aground. We figured the grinding noise was the new sonar dome, hanging below the hull being crushed. The bottom in the Block Island area is hard shale and difficult to set an anchor, the bow rising and falling with the swells must have pulled the anchor out of whatever it had a hold in. The drifting was so slow it went unnoticed by the watch on the bridge, they tried to reset the anchor by playing out more chain and slowly reversing the engine hoping the anchor would bite. The end of the chain in the locker had never been secured when the ship was built. They lost 150 fathoms of chain (450 feet) plus the anchor. The ship ran aground at high tide, when the tug boats arrived it was low tide, they could not budge the ship until the tide came in, about 11 PM that night. The island residents awoke to find a Navy warship parked in their bay. I found out you Yanks really do have a sense of humor, "Embarrassing." Now, off to dry dock for repairs, a lot of Liberty and 300 more poor sailors being chased by women. Ah, what us brave, good lookin, v-rile, hot blooded young seamen had to endure for our country. (This doesn't mean me honey, I wasn't on that ship.)

* * * * *

My duties as mailman on this size ship brought me into close contact with many of the crew. When they wrote those very special letters to their families, wives, or sweethearts back home, they knew I was the one who made sure those letters were put on their way to each of their loved ones. When those special letters came in, I was the one responsible for bringing them to the ship and very often putting them right into their hands. They seemed to accept me as being a part of their private lives. Our ship did not have a chaplain on board and when they had personal problems or just needed someone other than their friends to talk with, they would often come to me, especially the younger ones. I got to know them on a personal basis. I looked at many pictures of girlfriends, wives, babies, and families. Although I would never meet them, I knew the names of many of their girlfriends and wives. We laughed together during happy news, we cried together when things went wrong. There were sweethearts that wrote each other most every day. Privacy aboard a crowded ship does not exist, but each man had his own place to go and read his letter from that very special lady. I could see their disappointment when there was no letter for them and if this continued he would slowly change into an entirely different person, he was far at sea, no way to call home.

On a Navy ship, every morning, all hands must line up according to their division, for orders of the day and muster. If a man is missing he is reported as unaccounted for. If the ship is at sea an immediate search is begun. There have been cases when young sailors were listed as lost at sea; sometimes, the real truth was learned from the proverbial "Dear John" letter found in his locker. The Master At Arms or the Captain would order the lock to be cut to remove personal items to be sent to his family, most everything except the D.J. letter. I once had a chance to read one of those letters. "Dear --- This is a letter I never dreamed I would ever have to write to you, but I have no choice. I would rather you hear it from me than someone else. I told you two months ago about going to a dance with some friends and I did not have a date. I went just to have some fun with my friends. After the dance we all piled into two cars. I thought we were going to a drive in for snacks. A girl in the other car's parents own a cabin out by Lake ---, you and I have gone swimming there. I didn't mean for it to happen, but it did, my first and only time. I am going to have a baby." Up to this point the pages had been balled up and twisted in his sudden anguish. There were more pages which I did not see but those last words made him do whatever he did. I don't know if he straightened the pages out or if the Captain did when he had to read the letter. I believe it was the Captain's duty to write a personal letter to the family when something happened to a member of his crew. The details of something like this surely were never mentioned, I imagine the families had no problem figuring it out in this case. Hearts are broken both ways, young people whose bodies are changing, wanting to explore the mysteries of life. Not sure how to deal with the urges they feel or how to handle the temptations that are sure to come.

Those were some of the sad times but mostly it was work and fun times. As I have written before, the mailman was usually first or one of the first to go ashore because every man was waiting for letters from home. (No females were allowed aboard warships then. The women were needed on the home front and also were smart enough to let the men come home with the battle ribbons and be welcomed into their arms as their heroes for life.) Perhaps this is one of the reasons most marriages during that era were successful and lasted forever, yes, I said forever, death does not end a longtime, happy marriage.

* * * * *

There were times when my ship was assigned to and operated out of ports like Key West, Florida and Newport, Rhode Island. From these ports and others there were weeks of A.S.W. (Anti Submarine Warfare). I was involved very little in A.S.W. practice. This was the toughest part of my job, every guy on the ship felt sorry for me. While all the other guys were happily heading out to sea, they left me standing on the dock, tears in my eyes, watching my ship disappear over the horizon. They didn't need the mailman, "Sob-sniff". Finally, it was out of sight. Hubba hubba hoochie coo, lookout girls, lookout beaches, here comes da mailman, here comes da mailman. I had five whole days in the sun and surf and sand and four whole nights, -- wherever, to work up the terrific energy I would need for the one hour it would take to have the mail ready when my ship returned on Friday.

Just about everything in Key West was within walking distance. I was totally on my own, I slept in a barracks on the base, had breakfast in the mess hall, the post office was off base so I didn't need a gate pass. The Marines guarding the gate did wonder why I was returning so late at night carrying a mail pouch and not in dress uniform. I kept my swimming trunks, toothbrush, etc in the mail pouch, I could have slept on the beach if I wanted to but the beach and fishing and girls soon became tiresome. Now, I can't believe that last part. They had the best USO (United Service Organization) Club I have ever visited, sitting in a grove of palm trees surrounded by every type of tropical plants. I spent a lot of time there, mostly studying for my First Petty Officer rating. I received my first stripe and Eagle while in Key West. Third class Petty Officer.

* * * * *

We were based there about two months. During that time a hurricane started kicking up in the South Atlantic waters heading for the islands and tracking towards Key West. Ships like ours, if left tied to a dock during a strong hurricane, could batter the dock to pieces and damage the ship. When the time came, we sailed into The Gulf of Mexico to get out of its way or ride out the storm. It turned into The Gulf and we caught the full fury. It was "don't bar the barn door Nellie, the horse is already out." The waves were not as high as we had experienced but there were tornado like winds within the storm and it was difficult to keep the ship on course. I was manning radar at the time (the eyes of the ship) visibility was about zero. I picked up on the radar scope a large object in the water a few thousand feet away and closing in rapidly, either the ship was being blown toward the object, which was low in the water and intermittently would disappear from the radar scope, or it was moving in our direction. It soon came under the radar signal and completely vanished. All hands were alerted to the possibility of a collision. Tense moments passed and nothing happened. We figured it must have been a large barge (Oops – large barge) possibly upside down that the storm had blown into The Gulf. The Coast Guard was notified.

We returned to Key West to find the storm had turned further south and completely missed the island. We bid farewell to Key West, I really enjoyed my stay there. We did a bit of island hopping to Guantanamo Bay (Gitmo to you old salts) Cuba, sailed south to Trinidad – Tobago, Port of Spain for several weeks. We had hoped and were disappointed that we did not cross the equator we were so close, with all the fun (I guess) of the ancient sailing ships tradition of initiating those of the crew crossing the equator for the first time, into the inner sanctum of King Neptune. (Sorry old salts, I don't know all the correct words.)

We now sailed east for Atlantic Fleet exercises and then to Newport, Rhode Island for three weeks of some type of special training and A.S.W. Again, my General Quarters station, if needed, could be handled by others who were assigned to that position. Guess what!! The mailman remained ashore, only this time there was no Naval Base, I had an apartment in town and a special allowance for meals. I took a bus to a nice horse rental stable, close to the beach where I rode my horse. I loved riding and working with these critters. I even made some extra money helping at the stable during the day and slept there a couple of nights. But even Cinderella had time limits. I was back on my job when my ship returned on Friday evenings.

* * * * *

In my writing it may seem that a ships mailman is a darling of the Navy and given special privileges. Some of our duties by their very nature could be just that. I was Postmaster of a Third Class Post Office and served under the Postmaster General and Secretary of the Navy. Those long boat trips in every kind of weather and conditions to take care of the U.S. mail and guard mail could get very boring and sometimes treacherous, like Newfoundland where I nearly froze my hands and Greenland during the winter. The Navy and especially ship Captains know the importance of morale among their crew. During extended periods of time at sea and often very inclement weather conditions, tempers flared and mail not leaving or coming aboard made it worse. Most of those men lived to receive their letters from that someone very special to them. If the mailman remained ashore, when that ship docked or dropped anchor and that gangplank came down, he had better be on his way up with the mail sorted and ready to hand out to the different divisions for mail call or his butt just might get tossed overboard.

* * * * *

Butterfly! Butterfly was difficult to not notice, small of stature, a thin, peak nose and ears that grew straight out and bent forward like the corner of a page you mark by bending down. He was new aboard our ship with a name hard to remember so someone called him Butterfly because of his ears, and it stuck. He was a bit shy and a loner. When I was sorting mail in my post office, for some reason I began to notice he never received mail and I never saw him mail a letter. One of the crew's favorite gathering places was in the shade of the big guns on the fantail. He had never spoken to me before, but he kidded me about everyone's favorite joke about the mailman, reading postcards and unsealed love letters. During our following conversation I learned he was raised in an orphanage, he never knew his mother or father or any other family member. He would see his friends being adopted but no one wanted him. The orphanage was the only family he knew. This got to me, I mentioned it to my friend Pat, the ship's senior cook and he took it from there.

I don't remember Butterfly's real name but I did remember he had a birthday coming up. Pat's girlfriend, Katie, sent him a birthday card. When his real name was first called he didn't respond, a second time he suddenly realized his name was actually called, he jumped up, rushed to get his mail, holding it in the tips of his fingers as though it was hot. Went to his own private spot, opened it ever so carefully, not wanting to tear the envelope. Pat and I were both watching him. He read the card and note several times and then he looked up at Pat. I looked at Pat too and he had a big grin on his face and tears were rolling down that big galoot's cheeks. He later told me what Katie had written with the birthday card., using his real name: "Dear ----- my boyfriend Pat seems to have special people he chooses to have as friends, he told me you have a birthday soon and I just wanted to wish you a happy birthday and maybe we can write to each other sometimes, Katie." The next day his name was called again. He had a big grin on his face when he rushed up to get his mail. This time it was a letter and it was not from Katie, it was from her younger sister. By the time I later was transferred off the USS Ellison, I watched this young man change from a timid little mouse everyone picked on, to one who could laugh when they called him Butterfly and come right back with a name for them. I feel like I made a difference in his life.

* * * * *

Of all the training cruises we made into the Atlantic, this was to be the most memorable, eventful, and dangerous one of all. It stands out so vividly in my memory after more than sixty years because everything that happened, unknown to me at the time, played a part in God's intricate plan, along with the lives of many others, but eventually leading me to the wonderful lady with whom I was destined to spend the rest of my life.

The first ten days we were further south, operating in calmer seas with many other ships, participating in war games. Although the hot war was officially over, there were still countries that needed to see and feel the readiness and might of the U.S. Naval fighting forces close to their shores. Sending them a message to put up or shut up, when the "hourly plan for the day" was posted on our bulletin board, about our tenth day at sea, I learned our ship would be pulling alongside the "Battleship Missouri" for transferring personnel and mail. The ships were cruising side by side and about forty feet apart. While the crews were positioning the lines, I was waiting for the mail and supplies to come aboard. I noticed a crewman on the Missouri jump down from his gun mount and start waving his arms frantically, looking closer I recognized him as a friend of mine from an air base we were on. Here we were, meeting in the middle of the Atlantic Ocean, for the first time in nearly two years. All we could do was look at each other and wave. Soon the mail came across and I had to get busy. I never saw him again.

* * * * *

Medical facilities were very limited on a destroyer. During the fleet exercises a crewman on our ship came down with appendicitis. The hospital ship "Consolation" was a part of the fleet and had the facilities and doctors to perform the operation. Early the next morning, our ship prepared to transport the patient to the hospital ship. Port side, by Breeches Bouy, a covered seat with safety belt hung on a line above the water, and pulled to the receiving ship. This was exciting to every man on our ship in another way, we had not seen females for weeks. It's amazing how much a man craves and longs for just the clean, sweet smells of a woman. The upper decks on the hospital ship were two or three stories above our main deck. The WAVES, wearing skirts, had a bird's eye view of the action below while we had a worm's eye view watching them above. With all the extra weight, it's a wonder out ship didn't capsize to port. Boys will be boys you know, that's the way God made us.

* * * * *

During this cruise we anchored out from some islands, I believe it was the Azores where we were given Liberty ashore for a few days. This was also the first time we saw what we believed was female slave trade in action. A group of us went to a dance club for drinks and dancing with whatever girls were available. We started noticing some of the girls looked very young, 12-15 at the most. They all were wearing heels and short skirts, some, garter belts with tops of hose exposed and they would solicit us to buy drinks and go to rooms upstairs. One told us if she didn't make enough money they would put her out on the streets, which were very dangerous. We gave the girls some money but that's all we wanted. We also noticed men sitting by the exit doors. We guessed they were there to keep the girls from leaving. We learned later that pictures were taken of the girls performing with men and other girls in the rooms and sold in other markets. The club really was nice, but we had the feeling if we said anything there would be trouble for the girls and probably us. Some of us had young sisters, we expressed our concerns to the executive officer of our ship, second in command of most Navy ships. He said it was well known that this was going on in probably all of the major islands. The authorities were being well paid to look the other way. It continues today and maybe even more so.

* * * * *

During the remaining days of fleet maneuvers, we sailed further south, skirting due east of the Sargasso Sea area where hurricanes are born. The water was mirror smooth. 2400 o'clock, (midnight), I had just come off duty at my radar station. I was not sleepy, the temperature was pleasant, not a whisper of a breeze. No moon in the sky above and not a cloud could be seen. I walked aft to the fantail, found a bunk mattress, climbed the ladder to the top of the after 5"38 gun mount and lay down to a panoramic celestial view that defies all words of description. It was one of those rare moments, never seen by most people on earth, everything came together perfectly. An unobstructed, no manmade lights, non polluted, crystal clear night from horizon to horizon. It looked like there was a star every few inches and when I starred at any one spot for a while, I thought I could see twinkling even there. Unbelievably beautiful, awesome, breathtaking. I realize now, that was the only time in my life I could see 360°, horizon to horizon. Except for my ship, I could see absolutely nothing that was created by man, not even another human being. I imagined myself being only a comparative few thousand feet out in space, looking back at this same scene, even the 400 foot ship I was on would be only a tiny speck in the water and I would be invisible. I can never forget that night.

* * * * *

Now to the opposite extreme, it was a warm, sunny day, the water was choppy. As we sailed north, to the east, low on the horizon we could see dark clouds starting to appear. About an hour later we were still in bright sunshine, the water was rolling swells a bit higher now. Very dark, thick, roiling, menacing thunder heads tens of thousands of feet high were on the east horizon. We were all watching this drastic change. Our ship was still in bright sunlight, the dark clouds formed a definite line across the overhead sky. It went from blue sky to very dark, foreboding. As we sailed on, the rolling black clouds going down to the ocean became much denser and now black. We could see a very wide point where this entire mass seemed to squat right down on the water. We were watching an unusually large water spout. We had seen many small ones, a terrible tornado on the ocean. I have been told this is how God puts water into the clouds to carry rain water over his lands. The Captain wanted to report and observe this phenomenon for a while. Then, we sailed northward to join other destroyers for special exercises. Little did we know what lay ahead for us.

* * * * *

The further north we sailed, the more hostile the ocean became. The temperature dropped rapidly. We rendezvoused with the other three destroyers in our squadron along with supply ships, submarines and at least one cruiser in the frigid North Atlantic. I had to take my turn along with other crewmen battling the heavy formation of ice, especially on the bow area of the ship. About the third night into the north seas exercises, the night was very dark, the swells were running high, and the ship was taking about 60° rolls which was about normal for these waters. 0300 o'clock (morning) most of the crew was asleep, suddenly a loud crash, the entire ship shuddered, engines were reversed, everyone was awakened expecting the general quarters alarm, scrambling to the main deck to see what had happened, no alarm was sounded. We had collided with another ship. A seaman on lookout duty spotted the ship cresting a wave above us, he said it looked like the other ship was going to come down right on top of ours but as the wave moved under the ship it seemed to pull back and came down for a glancing blow to our starboard bow area, taking out our lifelines, a life raft, and other minor damage that a paint brush could fix, but it sure woke everyone up.

I'm not sure how it all came out, if we were off course or if it was the other ship and why wasn't it picked up on radar? After sixty-three years I don't remember the answers. I do remember the chiefs were a bit bleary eyed during the next day. Their quarters were at the exact point of impact. There were a few bruises, jangled nerves, and broken after shave lotion bottles. The most exciting and dangerous was still to come. I don't want to leave the impression that the North Atlantic is always extremely rough, we had very good days. But we were not ordered up there for a pleasure cruise, our mission was deadly serious. Most any man can be a fair weather sailor but a real "Tin Can Sailor" is a different breed. Big ship admirals have said they would not go into battle or sail a convoy without "The Cans". From their very beginning history, destroyers were designed to be fighting ships. During and after WWII, it seems our most important function was "ASW", Anti Submarine Warfare practice. We all had a job to do, and we did them well, each man's life could very well depend on how the next man performed his job. This had been proven many times during actual battles. Most WWII destroyers were 390-400 feet long, depending on the class, with 300 crewmen and 25 officers. There were about 200 men in the after crews quarters. You might say a very close knit society but it did get a little crowded in the head (bathroom) at times.

* * * * *

When we arrived on station the ships had taken a pretty good pounding from the high seas, we could not take on provisions, and the exercises were cancelled. Our next operational destination we were really looking forward to was Key West, Florida again, but for now we were still in the stormy North Atlantic. Luckily, this destroyer had inside passageways forward and aft, we did not have to race the waves on the weather deck as the ship rolled from side to side. Early, during our first night heading south, something very heavy hit the deck just over our heads. We could hear it rolling back and forth across the fantail of the ship. The depth charges, weighing hundreds of pounds, were stored in elevated, enclosed, brackets with tracks inside. The depth charge itself, oval shaped like a big fat football with hoop like wheels welded to each end, when the ship was tracking a suspected or known enemy submarine, the depth charges were set to explode at different depths where the sub was thought to be. The depth charges were stored in the brackets and rolled down the tracks where they could be dropped one at a time into the water from each side of the ship. As I understand, the ship needed to be making 20-30 knots of speed to get away from the force of the explosion and high geyser of water.

By now we had been in very heavy seas for more than six days. The constant roll from side to side caused one of the heavy depth charges to loosen and gradually knock out a side brace and work its way out, fell to the deck and began rolling from side to side. It didn't take but a few rolls for it to knock out the lifelines and plunge into the water. Because of the weather, the ship could make only about five knots. The time between hitting the deck and the explosion was about thirty seconds. The after part of the ship was lifted out of the water, that's where most of the crew was berthed and that's where I was. Those of us not in our bunks who were standing on the deck, felt like our feet were burned from the force of the explosion but no one was hurt. Since the depth charges rolled on a track, the next one rolled into its place. It took about half an hour for each of the two remaining charges at that point in line to work its way out. The charges were not set for any particular depth when two of the three exploded under our ship, but all of this did split the seams in the hull and we were taking on water. There was nothing we could do about the problem because sea water was washing deep across the weather deck with every roll of the ship. The damage control crew did a great job of securing the breaks but instead of sunny Key West, Florida, we were now bound for dry dock at the Charleston, South Carolina shipyards with a short stop over at Bermuda. We took a lot of kidding about trying to blow ourselves up.

* * * * *

Coming from the frigid north seas, Bermuda was a very welcome, pleasant place to stop. We were there five or six times so I don't remember when the following things took place. For the first time I was given "Shore Patrol" duty (police). There I was, all lanky, six foot 135 pounds of me, when the wind blew hard I could stand sideways and the wind didn't touch me. All decked out with leggings laced up around the bottoms of my pant legs, an "S.P." band around the top of one of my sleeves, I had a problem making both letters show.

Too much band, not enough arm. White hat squared up on my head where I never wore it but regulations required. A long "Billy Club" put in my hand. If a fight broke out in a bar or dance hall we were to wade in and break it up. Luckily, Bermuda had very few of these, but I did get a chance to exercise my authority once.

There were only two Navy ships anchored out at the time and a short narrow road led to the boat dock for Liberty boats back to the ships. We S.P.s had a jeep to sit in to watch the sailors returning to their ship. I noticed one young sailor staggering back to his ship. I stood up, with my feet wide apart, staring at him, bumping my Billy Club into the palm of my hand "Barney Fife style" and said in my most commanding voice, "Straighten up there sailor," it worked, he suddenly wasn't drunk anymore. I turned around with a proper sneer on my face, looked at my fellow "S.P.s" plopped down in my seat, still bumping my club in the palm of my hand. That was the first and last time I was given shore patrol duty.

* * * * *

Bermuda, on the map or globe, is just a tiny dot about 600 miles into the Atlantic, east of South Carolina, the northern most point of the mysterious Bermuda Triangle which we sailed many times. A close group of islands made up of tops of mountains in the deep Atlantic Ocean. The widest point across is about twenty miles, beautiful white sandy beaches, an average temperature of 65-75°. We were surprised the first time we asked for a glass of water in a restaurant and were charged five cents. I don't know about now but at that time there was no fresh water on the islands, only rainwater. As I remember, most or all of the homes, most buildings, and many hill tops were topped with a coral type material designed to catch and direct rainwater down into underground cisterns, serving as their only freshwater supply. The second thing most sailors did when their ship sailed into a seaport new to them was explore and see the area. In Bermuda, the most available building material seemed to be coral, not strong enough to hold heavy vehicles. A group of us hired a horse drawn tour wagon. We were plodding along a narrow coral road between two tree covered hills. In the cloudless sky above, we could see something very large in the distance that looked like it was sitting right on top of the green trees with the blue sky behind. As we drew closer and not at an angle, we could now see large letters coming into view, the first letter was a very large "N". The next letter was an "A", the next an "M", then we could read all of the sign, one word, "Hillman". I yelled look guys!! "I made it, my name in heaven." No one including me knew what it meant. The driver of our tour wagon knew what it meant but was not very pleased. He angrily explained that for the first time, Bermuda was allowing automobiles on the island and that the "Hillman" was a small car, light enough for transportation and not to do very much damage to the coral roadbeds. I tried but never saw a "Hillman Car" until years later when they were brought to the U.S.

* * * * *

The third day we sailed out of Bermuda bound for repairs at dry dock in Charleston, South Carolina. I probably will never see Bermuda again. Little did I realize all of this was in preparation for putting all the final parts together for me to find the girl I would spend my life with. Within the next few months, our paths would finally cross, each of us at the exact same spot on earth at the same second, for our eyes to meet and see the person that God had created for each one, since birth, to meet and mate and love for life.

While our ship was being repaired in Charleston, they gave those of us who lived in the near eastern states ten days leave. This was the first time I could go home in more than a year. A time to really relax, sleep late, and have breakfast any time of the day. The ten days passed too quickly. This was the time before the big airlines. I boarded a workhorse of the Air Force, a C-47 cargo plane, converted to hauling paying passengers. I was flying to Charleston, South Carolina by way of Jacksonville, Florida, a few landings in between just above or right through the cloud cover, no high altitude flights. The "barf bags" were in heavy use, even I, a seasoned rough seas sailor felt a bit queasy. The gung-ho stewardess was determined to do her job, serve a meal. Some couldn't eat, others settled for a roll from the pan she could carry. Everyone applauded and thanked her for her efforts as they left the plane. Today, I hear spoiled brats complain about the movie, magazines or being a few minutes late. After that flight, I was happy to get back to joy riding in fifty foot seas twenty-four hours a day.

* * * * *

During the time our ship was in dry dock for repairs, we often had extra shore Liberty. A group of us who pal'd around together committed one of our biggest "boo-

boos, ooops" or whatever, and this time it wasn't girls, cards, or tying knots. We liked to ride horses rented from a nearby stable. There were several great riding trails we really enjoyed and had fun, sometimes riding until well after dark. One of those nights the moon was very bright but thick clouds would drift by. It was like flipping a switch and turning out the light in a dark room. There were eight of us talking and walking our horses back to the stables. A cloud shut off the moonlight and we were letting the horses follow the trail. But horses, on their own, do not follow man made trails. By instinct, they follow the shortest route to wherever they are going. We started hearing strange, plopping, squishing sounds and it was not the horses raising their tails all at the same time. As the cloud cover moved on we could see round, shiny things all around us. "Oh boy," watermelons, eight horses, thirty-two horse hooves walking through a melon patch in the dark. What a "revoltin situation this was." We turned the horses around, trying our best to follow the same path back as we came in. Only a short way we found the work gate someone left open and the horses had passed through. We did the best we could but I'm sure glad we were not there when the farmer found his melon patch trampled. Knowing whoever left those gates open was really at fault helped ease our conscience a bit, no we did not sample any of the melons.

* * * * *

The other three destroyers in our squadron were at Key West, Florida. We were looking forward to joining them but the Lord had other plans. I am not sure why we were ordered to Hampton Roads at Norfolk, something to do with sonar and another piece of our equipment. We arrived sometime in July or early August. The crew still thought we would be going to Key West, but that was not to be, and if you had told me I would be out of the Navy by Christmas, I would have said, "No way Hosea", bit of Spanish lingo there, hope I spelled it right. I was still a hot blooded young sailor, looking for something wearing a skirt. If you think that's crude just think of the alternative, I'm not that kind of angel. Just kidding Honey, just kidding.

In my personal experience with the men on my two ships, I knew who had wives and sweethearts back home and I would see some of their conduct while they were ashore. I am sure they would not want their ladies doing the same things with other men. I was certainly not perfect, but neither was I married, committed, or seriously involved with any girl before I met my Katherine. Good role models had a way of coming into my life at the right time. I like to refer to them as my "Guardian Angels" because it seems they were in and out of my life at just the right times to guide me in the right direction at that point of my maturity and age. I have brought them in all through these writings.

* * * * *

The ships I served on where we lived in very close quarters, there would have been over 700 men that in some way may have influenced my life in one way or another. Now, more than sixty years later, only one stands out in my memory while on ships. He was a petty officer first class, three stripes under the eagle on his sleeve, he was the head cook on the ship I was on the longest time. I can remember only his first name, "Pat", he had a very special sweetheart, "Katie". Her picture was the only one on his locker door. I don't believe there was a day, seven days a week, that a letter did not come in for him and one go out for her. I used to kid him about being my best customer, buying whole sheets of stamps at a time.

Because of space, physical activity was limited aboard the ship. When our ship was in port, instead of heading out to the bars, night clubs, or dance hall, I would see Pat jogging around the base streets or working out in the gym. He was the type of man others would look up to and when he put on his uniform, although not what you would call overly handsome, he was a good, solid man that made the girls take a second look, but he had eyes only for his Katie. When we went on Liberty together he liked movies, stage shows, riding horses, and sightseeing, nothing that involved women. He was absolutely true to Katie. We became very good friends. He was with us in Charleston, South Carolina when our eight horses wandered into the farmer's watermelon field. When we were at sea, since he was head cook, some nights he would fix special snacks, we would go to my mail shack, close the door, eat and spend time just talking.

One day he came down and had a puzzled look on his face, he asked me if I knew of anyone whose initials were M.M. I asked him why? Somebody is putting little notes on the back side of the envelope with my letters to Katie with the initials M.M. I suggested it must be someone who knows her at your local post office. Several days later he brought some of the envelopes she received and said she checked with her

P.O. and no one there had those initials. I read the notes, "Hi Katie M.M. – Hope you are well Katie M.M. – Have a nice day Katie M.M. – Later he brought more envelopes, the mystery deepens for the lovers, who is this culprit? Is he breaking the postal laws? I checked the rules book, no laws broken. This went on for several weeks, it was driving him crazy. He told me, "I believe Katie is getting more excited about those little notes than my letters. I said it has to be somebody in your post office or your mailman. On the last envelope were the words "Horses and watermelons. M.M." I asked, "What does that mean?" I knew exactly what it meant. I wanted to see how long I could keep it going. But when he got that bewildered expression, I could not hold it in any longer. When I turned around and pretended to sort some mail, suddenly he grabbed my collar, turned me around, his face reddened, put a finger in my face, gritting his teeth and said, "I want you, right now, to let me see you write the letters." M.M. (= mailman = mystery man = Wally Hillman.)

I wrote the words "Horses and watermelons – M.M." just like the words that were on the envelope. His mouth opened, his eyes wide, he sat down in his chair and we both had a "real belly bustin laugh." When he told Katie, she said for me to keep it up, the first thing she looked for was her mystery message. We became pen pals on the back of their envelopes.

* * * * *

After being at sea for several weeks, during September 1947, late on a Saturday afternoon, my ship returned to Norfolk. By the time we arrived at our anchorage station, dropped anchor and secured the ship, I decided to stay on board and go ashore the next day, Sunday. I was lying in my bunk reading when one of my best buddies, Andy, grabbed my legs, pulled them over the side and said, "Get dressed, I've got to feel dry land for a change and I don't want to go by myself." It was a twenty minute boat trip to the fleet landing. We stopped in a small night club nearby for a few beers and were approached by a couple of prostitutes; there were always plenty of them around to take care of sailors who have been at sea for awhile. The Navy makes it very clear the consequences of playing around with these ladies. If you get more than you pay for and end up in sick bay and cannot work, just as with a sunburn you will be court marshaled and punished with loss of pay and restriction to base or ship until you can perform your regular duties.

    We rode a trolley car into downtown Norfolk, paid fifty cents each for a couple of bunk beds at the "Navy Y". Nearby was the C.P.O. Club (Chief Petty Officers) a privately owned club, but sponsored by the Navy as I understand it. No admission charge, the drinks were cheap, and on the weekends had a dance band. During the week, dance music on a juke box. The "Shore Patrol" (Navy Police) was always present to keep order. When you mix sailors – cocktails – and women there is bound to be a few problems. Keep in mind we were living in another era, time, place, and people were different, we thought different, we acted different. Drugs as we know them today were nonexistent. Girls dressed like girls, acted like girls, were taught girl things. Boys looked like boys, acted like boys, were taught boy things.

Because of the war, all able bodied men from age eighteen up were subject to being called into the military. This left many jobs normally performed by men unfilled. Women of all ages began leaving the farms, small towns, and rural area going to the larger cities, playing a very important role in filling positions in industry, offices, hospitals, sales, manufacturing, everything needed to keep war materials moving. This meant most young people were away from home. Men and women scattered all over the country, all over the world. Young people have a way of finding each other.

This was also the era of "Big Bands" forming to play dance tunes of the time. The music was soft, in the background, romantic or fast, you could have a good time talking at your table or whispering sweet nothings to each other while dancing. Tens of thousands of young women were away from home working these jobs, sharing living quarters in homes, boarding houses, dormitories, the Y.W.C.A., etc. It <u>was not</u> frowned upon when groups of them got all dressed up, did what girls do to make themselves beautiful, and went to a dance hall as a group, safety in numbers, where they knew many young sailors, soldiers, marines, etc. would be. These young men too, had been called away from the farms, small towns, and big cities. Most were teenagers or early twenties, all looking for an evening of fun. By the end of the evening, many had paired off, dates were made, and telephone numbers were exchanged. The guys walked the girls home, holding hands, talking, and hoping for a goodnight kiss. (Very few had cars.)

All of this certainly has its downside. Every city of any size has its share of those ready and willing to supply the erotic needs of humans. The mobsters, pimps, and girls of the night who go where the men are to ply their trade and many of them can make themselves very attractive. They may have daytime jobs but they hustle at night and since they need men, they too were at these dances mingling with the decent girls. It didn't take long for the guys to know who they were. They made dates by the hour, the word passed around, most of them left these girls alone but after a few drinks some just didn't care and went with them.

There were several clubs like this in the Norfolk area, but this one was known throughout the fleet. Word was passed from ship to ship, if your ship goes into Hampton Roads, the place to find the most and best women is the downtown Norfolk CPO Club. Secretaries, store sales girls, nurses and college girls flock to that club. My shipmate and I had been there several times before and we knew some of the girls. We sat at their table, had a few dances. We were tired from a long day so we went back to the "Navy Y" for some sleep. Little did I dream that the next morning, something wonderful was going to happen that would literally change my life forever.

Sunday morning, 10:00 AM, a warm, sunny, September day, Andy and I stepped out onto the streets of Norfolk, looking for a place to have breakfast. 1947, Sunday, the Sabbath was well observed, most businesses were closed but drug stores were open seven days a week. We noticed a Whelan Drug Store with a lunch counter just down the street. We went into a side door near the back, sat at a table next to and talked with an elderly couple who had a grandson on a ship out in the bay. At that moment, my life changed forever when I looked up and saw the prettiest and, to me, the most beautiful girl I had ever seen, coming to take our orders. Suddenly, bells began to ring, my heart beating faster, my face flushed, my mouth wide open. I must have had a stupid expression on my face because Andy was laughing and said, "What the hell is wrong with you?" Andy and I had been in most every seaport around the Atlantic, the Caribbean, and into the Norwegian Sea and Arctic Ocean but I had never had a girl affect me like this. It was love at first sight for me. She was tall, slender, natural honey blonde, wavy hair and a figure that just wouldn't quit. She took our orders and left. I said to Andy, "Boy, I would really like to date her!!" He said, "Well, why don't you do what you <u>always</u> do? <u>Ask</u> her." When she returned, I asked if she would have dinner with me sometime. She said, "OK," turned and walked away. I was just another flirty sailor to her. I made the mistake of saying <u>sometime</u> instead of a definite time.

  I went there for my usual bacon and egg breakfast but could not remember what I actually ordered until fifty some years later when we were reading a letter I had written during our courtship. The waitresses were having a contest that day. The one who sold the most "banana splits" would win a prize. That's right, she took advantage of my condition. Instead of my bacon and eggs, she sold me a banana split for breakfast. She won the contest. I guess if the contest had been selling marmalade sandwiches I would have eaten a dozen marmalade sandwiches, which I hated. For more than fifty years I could not remember what we did after leaving the store. Now I do remember. That vision of loveliness was very busy waiting on other customers. Andy and I left the store and visited a nearby church. I later learned it was the same church the lady who had taken my heart attended. After church we walked to a nearby park that had a nice lake, a lot of ducks and other birds. This was a sunny, warm day in September of 1947 and the trees were starting their fall colors. Again, we later learned it was a nice little park that Katherine and her friends often spent the day enjoying.

* * * * *

Our ship was scheduled to go back to sea early the next morning so Andy and I took the trolley back to the base, went to the fleet landing, and the Liberty boat took us back to our ship. From then on, that pretty blonde lady's face was there on my mind. I could not stop thinking about her. Somehow, I knew she was going to be more than just another pretty face to me and I didn't even know her name. I'm not sure how long we were at sea this time, usually a week or ten days. Although the fighting war was over, the Cold War was in full swing. The Russian Communist dictator, Joseph Stalin, was angered by President Roosevelt's outsmarting him. As I understand it, on "D-Day", when the Allies crossed the English Channel to invade Europe, Stalin had the understanding the U.S. would send troops to help the Russians fight the Germans from the east. No troops were sent and the Russians had to do their own fighting. They were now developing their own atomic bombs and other weapons so the United States had to remain on high alert status. Since the troops and equipment were already in place,

General George Patton wanted to go ahead and take care of the Russians. I think he was right but the politicians would not hear of this. Also, the Koreans were causing problems. The Cold War heated up.

After seeing Katherine for the first time, as I remember, my ship and others sailed out of Hampton Roads bound for training exercises and maneuvers in the North Atlantic. If we were going to fight the Russians, this is where a lot of the sea action would take place. This is also where a sailor finds out if he is man enough to really be a "Tin Can Sailor". Destroyers were always my first choice and I am proud to be called a Tin Can Sailor. Guys on aircraft carriers said that during really rough seas they could see the Destroyers only about one third of the time. The other two thirds, they disappeared in the trough between monstrous waves. They wondered if we were going to come back up.

* * * * *

Sometime during September 1947, my ship returned to Norfolk on a Saturday afternoon. After the ship is anchored and secure, normally the mailman is among the first ashore to fleet post office and take care of outgoing and incoming mail, then to the motor pool to check out a vehicle assigned to the ship, return to the ship, sort and disburse mail. It was now time for evening meal. I ate aboard ship, put on my dress uniform, and ran to the quarter deck just in time to catch the Liberty boat to the fleet landing. I had anxiously thought about this moment the entire time we were at sea. I had gone through all of this many times except this time was different because this girl did something to me that had never happened before.

Now I was heading for the one I love, the lady who really got my attention that Sunday morning serving me a "banana split" breakfast two weeks before. On the trolley into town I was so anxious and nervous I was sweating on a chilly September evening. I had practiced all of my tried and true approaches. Would she be there – would she talk to me – would she brush me off – would she even notice me – would she be going steady with someone – as pretty as she is, she must be engaged, maybe she is married? By this time the trolley stopped right across the street from her drug store, believe it or not I was really kind of a shy guy around some girls but never to this extent. I walked to the front door and stopped. I decided to peep in the window hoping to see her again but could not see much of the store. I went in, didn't see her, I described her to one of the girls, she was not working that night and the girl would not tell me her name. A very, very disappointed young sailor walked out of that store.

The C.P.O. Club was just a few blocks away so I decided to go there. As I told you earlier, I had been to this club before and had met and dated several of the girls, it was really a fun place to go. The large dance hall was on the second floor, there was a live band on Friday and Saturday nights and usually was crowded. I walked up the long, wide stairway to the dance floor. The girls I already knew sat at their favorite table. I made my way through the crowd and said hello to my friends. Suddenly, there she was, she took my breath. Her golden hair shining like a halo under the dimmed lights, wearing a pretty, black cocktail dress, even more beautiful than my dreams, my imagination, or thoughts had pictured her while I was at sea. My heart dropped, even though I knew, during these times of war, young women working jobs away from home would go in groups to these clubs for an evening of fun dancing with the service men. I also knew this club was told by sailors from ship to ship as the place to go to find a better class of women, and men do tell tales and brag about their conquests.

Of the five girls at the table, I had dated two. Katherine worked with them at the drug store. In a letter I had written during our courtship, we read fifty some years later, I mentioned dancing with each of them before one of them introduced me to her. My "Guardian Angel again", the only empty chair at the table was right beside Katherine. I asked if she would mind me sitting there. We danced every dance with each other the rest of the evening. Even though I had just met her, I had never before enjoyed being with someone as much as I did with her. About an hour before the club was to close, I was surprised when the girl who introduced us asked if I would take Katherine home and to leave right then. What I am going to tell you next may shock you, but keep in mind we are talking about Katherine and I did not really know her at this point. I had been through similar routines before and although I thought she was the loveliest girl I had ever met, as we were holding hands and walking down the stairs, I was expecting to be propositioned and expecting her to tell me that her place was several miles away and we would have to take a cab, and if I wanted to we could spend the night there or there were places along the way. As we neared the bottom she was several steps ahead of me. She turned, took my hand, looked up at me with those big beautiful smiling eyes, sparkling from the lights overhead, and with her soft, southern voice, said words that nearly made my heart explode with sheer delight. She said, "come on, I don't live far and we can have fun walking." We held hands, we talked, we kidded each other, she bumped me with her hip and knocked me off the sidewalk but the best was yet to come.

Side note – I had never told Katherine about my thoughts as we left the club that night until she read this part nearly sixty years later. Her reaction? "She looked up at me, her eyes narrowed, she said, 'What would your answer have been if I really did proposition you that night???'" Oops – hadn't thought about that – Gulp – No matter which way I answer I am in deep trouble for a long time. Uh – Honey, how much longer you gonna sleep in the other room???

We had walked about six blocks when she said, "This is where I live." I looked up and the sign read Y.W.C.A. Young Womens Christian Association. This topped it all off. Not only was she even more than I had imagined and dreamed of before I actually met her, I learned she was also a wonderful Christian girl. She left the dance early because the weekend curfew at the "Y" was 1 o'clock. We had time for me to go inside to one of two old time parlors where we could sit, hold hands, and talk. Oh yes, the house mother would stroll through ever so often. My heart told me that this girl was going to be very important in my life. We made plans to go to the nearby park and movie the next day for our first date. A little holding hands, quick kiss, and

I was out the door. I don't believe I even had to walk down the steps. I was way up on cloud nine and so giddy I couldn't stand myself. I just could not believe how all of this had turned out, I actually had a date with her.

I walked back to the "Navy Y" where I had a bunk to sleep on but I was so excited I could not sleep. It just would not sink in I had actually spent a wonderful evening with her. She seemed to like me and she even gave me a date for the next day. I believe I was afraid to go to sleep, afraid I would wake up and find it was only a dream. I walked for a while, went back to the lobby and read until way into the morning, no TV back then. I finally got some sleep, until about noontime on Sunday.

This time, even though it was lunch time, I got my bacon and eggs. While I was eating, the older lady who cooked my breakfast came up to me and asked if I was from Roanoke? Turned out, Roanoke was also her home. She knew my mother and other members of my family. Her name was Hortense, I told her about meeting one of her waitresses at the club the night before and that we had a date that afternoon. She laughed and accused me of being a fast worker. She also said that Katherine was one of her favorites and a really nice, sweet girl. Since Hortense knew my family, she answered my questions and told me a lot about Katherine. I mentioned with her looks she had to be popular with the guys and was she going steady with any one of them? She said, "Yes, she is popular with the guys but I don't know that she is dating any particular one right now." (Boy, was that good to hear!) She also told me Katherine had been working at the store about one year and she knew only good things about her. Some of the other girls were jealous because of her blonde hair and their boyfriends would talk about it. She had never known of her doing anything she would not want others to know about like some of the girls.

I told Hortense about the Sunday morning I came in for breakfast and what happened to me when I first saw her. How I could not stop thinking and dreaming about her while I was at sea. How extremely disappointed I was when I found her at the "CPO Club", and how quickly that all changed when I walked with her to the Y.W.C.A. She laughed and said, "It is true, many of the girls who go there are looking for guys for other <u>reasons</u>, but you found one of the others. If I were a boy, Katherine is the kind of girl I would want to take home to my family." The more Hortense talked, the more excited I became. I just couldn't wait for two o'clock to come so I could be with her again.

* * * * *

We had a wonderful time at the park, window shopping, having dinner, going to the movie, and slowly walking the long way, holding hands, back to the Y.W.C.A. My ship was in port for the next four days. Katherine and I had two more dates, giving us time to get to know each other a little better. The other two days I was on duty and had to stay on board. The fifth day we went to sea again. When we returned, Katherine had gone home to Carolina for the three days we were in port and I didn't get to see her. What a miserable three days I had. She returned the same day we were going back to sea for about two weeks. While on this cruise an announcement was made on the ships intercom that we were in the area where the Titanic had gone down. This time we knew the cruise was not going to be a picnic, we were heading straight to the North Atlantic and this was also hurricane season. The High Command had intentionally picked the most severe weather conditions possible for special training the crews in performing our duties at battle stations during extremely adverse weather conditions.

With the heavy dual "Five inch Thirty Eight" gun mounts and other topside equipment, Destroyers tended to be a bit top-heavy. While maintaining course into monster waves, the ship's roll from side to side caused many anxious moments, experienced seamen know what it is like to take salt water down the stack. The maximum roll of a Destroyer is about seventy-two (degrees), beyond that, the ship is likely to roll onto its side and sink. Example: a circle has 360 degrees, if you dip a round time clock half way down into a container of water, the water level would be at three and nine o'clock. That would mean 180° is under water and 180° is above water. If a Destroyer is in calm water, the mast is pointing to twelve o'clock – if the ship is in rough water and the mast is pointing over to twelve minutes til or after twelve o'clock it is near its maximum roll and may go to lying on its side and sinking. Time has nothing to do with any of the above; I'm just using the clock and minutes instead of degrees to make it easier to understand. (I hope.) Only the Bridge Crew knew the actual degree of roll, the rest of us were busy at our General Quarters (Battle) stations, but we knew the ship was taking some very long rolls.

During the terrible Okinawa Typhoon in December 1944 where parts of massive aircraft carrier's flight decks were ripped off, two Destroyers actually rolled over during the night. Another broke in half, taking the lives of almost the entire crews of over 300 men on each ship. The next morning those three ships had simply vanished. As I remember there were few survivors. Just as the crewmen on those Destroyers, we were wearing our life jackets twenty-four hours a day and sleeping topside wherever we could find enough space to sit or lie down even on the hard, steel deck. Sleeping in our regular quarters below deck, you had very little chance of surviving a rollover. We had been in high seas many times but never before was it like this.

* * * * *

Maneuvers over, we sailed back to Norfolk, after a two day stay in Bermuda. It was cool there but what a relief to be away from the frigid far North Atlantic. I enjoyed Bermuda very much each time we put in there, but this time my mind was on something else, and I was anxious to return to Norfolk to see a very special lady. We had been at sea for about sixteen days and only one time, because of extreme weather conditions, could we send out or receive mail. I received a nice letter from Katherine. It was typed, I didn't like that, but better than no letter at all. Nothing really special because we had known each other for such a short time, but that letter meant more to me than she could have imagined. I must have read it a dozen times and kissed it every time during the two day cruise back to

Norfolk. We did not realize these letters would be the first of more than a hundred for each of us.

After we secured the ship at anchor, my paying job began. I joined the mailmen from other Destroyers that had sailed with us, in the motor launch to fleet landing to send out and pick up mail. I called Katherine at Whelan's Drug Store. She did not have a date planned, she said she was really happy I was back and yes, she would go to a movie with me that night. I was back on cloud nine again. Since Katherine and I sincerely believe God planned and blessed our marriage even before we were born, why did He arrange for me to meet her for the first time in a crowded dance hall where sailors go to meet women? When I think back to that night, as nervous as I was when I went into the drug store to see her again, a number of not good things could have happened. She could have been too busy to notice me. I may have chickened out and walked away, bought things I didn't really want, like the banana split breakfast when I first saw her, said something dumb that could have turned her off, or been just another flirty sailor trying to make time with the good looking blonde. A lot of other things including, being stomped into the dust by her six foot nine, three hundred pound boyfriend waiting for her to get off work. None of this happened of course and there was no boyfriend. That was just not the place for us to meet. The short walk and cool air to the popular dance club took away my jitters and provided something else that only He could have arranged, the only empty chair at the table was right beside the lady who stopped me dead in my tracks. My life was totally changed forever.

* * * * *

During mid November 1947, my ship returned early in the week, this was unusual but I am sure glad it did. After taking care of my duties as mailman, I called the drug store to talk with Katherine. The voice on the other end of the line said, "Wally, I've got bad news, she was rushed to DePaul Hospital earlier with severe pains, we think it is appendicitis but we have not heard anything yet." I was in a phone booth at the fleet post office. After weeks of hearing only male voices, I really looked forward to hearing her soft, sweet, feminine voice. This was a shock to me. I realized I was really in love with this lady. As I look back over the events of the time, I am even more convinced that this was another part in "Gods perfect plan" for Katherine and me to become as one and share our life together. I was now aboard my second ship, The USS Ernest G. Small. I cannot recall ever returning to port, at a time other than the end of the week after a training cruise, and especially on the same day Katherine became ill. I cannot consider it to be a coincidence. It was no longer a usual day, I just couldn't speed things up enough. When we return to port at the same time, all of the mailmen are picked up by a motor launch and taken to fleet landing. The other guys wanted to go to the ships store for a milkshake. I told them what had happened and talked them into returning right away.

In Norfolk, at that time, there was a long trolley car line from downtown Norfolk to Ocean View, the trolley went right by DePaul Hospital and close to Navy fleet landing. After my shipboard duties, everyday, I was on the trolley going to the hospital. Today an appendicitis operation is normally a simple, buttonhole procedure. In 1947, it was a more serious, five inch incision and a weeklong recovery time in the hospital. The patient was put to sleep by putting a mask over their nose and mouth and drops of ether on the mask. This was effective but the patient always woke up sick and throwing up. The ether smell sometimes sickened visitors.

When I first arrived at the hospital, she was mostly over the sick period but very weak and confused. This was her first time in a hospital and she was all alone with strangers. No family nearby, no one to tell her friends at the Y.W.C.A., only a few co-workers at the drug store, and "Happy Day" none of her other boyfriends thank you Lord, thank you, thank you, thank you. The word slowly spread, some of her girlfriends at the "Y" and co-workers at the drug store came to see her.

Our faith is strong, when we reminisce and our thoughts venture back to this time, we both firmly believe that God provided these moments for us to get to know each other in a more personal, intimate way. Since she had no family nearby and friends dropped by only occasionally, I was the only one there for her every day. The nurses noticed this and when I passed their station, they would make happy little comments, "Katherine is better today Wally, and we have her looking pretty for you." They were so right. I would shiver with anticipation as I approached her room. The nurses had prepared pillows so she could sit up. To me, the most beautiful doll would pale in comparison beside her. Each day when I saw her, my heart felt like it was going to pound right out of my chest. She wore a sky blue gown, her honey blonde hair, cupid bow red lips and sparkling eyes looking at me were almost more than I could handle. I just wanted to put my arms around her, kiss her, and hold her tight and never let go. I was truly in love with her.

When we first met, she figured she was a little older than me, so she took a year off her age of twenty-three. I figured she was a little older than me, so I added a year to my age of twenty. We both had to confess when we signed our marriage license. In those days it seems hospital rooms were made for convenience, not comfort. This room had high ceilings with a single, glaring bulb hanging down. The second night, one of Katherine's favorite nurses came in, looked at the light and said, "That light is so unromantic," she left the room and came back with a nice little lamp with a shade. Katherine and I were beginning to feel comfortable with each other. Since I did not have a car, before this, we could never really be alone together. Everything we did always involved other people. Even in the parlor at the "Y", other people, including the house mother, were always passing by. This was our first chance to really get to know each other.

Each day as I walked down the hall past the nurse's station I could tell by their faces and the little comments they made, they knew we were falling in love. I learned later they would go to her room before I arrived with mirrors for her to put on her makeup, helped her brush her hair just right, and arrange pillows so she could sit up. I believe she was almost as anxious to see me as I was to see her. I started rubbing and massaging her feet. This was the first time I had touched her in any way except when dancing, holding hands, or when my arms were around her when we kissed good night. The first time my fingernails touched her dainty little feet. I found out she is very ticklish on the bottom of them. Soon, I could rub and massage her neck and upper back, making her feel better. As a young Christian girl, brought up in a strict, proper family by loving parents, it took her a while to accept my love, to feel the touch of my hands, and trust my caresses, my intentions and treating her as a woman. I rejoiced and respected her for all of these things. She was beginning to see me as someone more than just another guy wanting a date with a pretty girl.

* * * * *

She was discharged from the hospital, after eight days. She was not ready to make the trip to her home in North Carolina and could not walk up three flights of stairs to her room at the "Y". One of her girlfriends at the drug store, knowing she would need a place other than the "Y" to stay until she could make the trip to her home, offered to share her room where she lived with her brother and sister-in-law. They welcomed and took good care of her. She has always been a sweet, likeable person. Margaret, the sister-in-law, and Katherine became great friends. I went to see her every night and became good friends of the brother and his wife. As I look back now, I realize they had to have been an extremely tolerant couple to allow me to come every might and use their living room to court Katherine. Sometimes I did not leave until one or two in the morning. Since television was unknown to us, I often wonder what we did all that time and even then, she had to run me out. By the time I got back to my ship I had about three hours to sleep before reveille. The next night, same thing, for ten days. I guess the Lord, in all his wisdom, does not bother to give us good common sense at twenty years of age. I did sleep in on the weekends.

Again, my "Guardian Angel" was there for me, when my ship returned from sea on the day Katherine had her operation. We were still an active, fully armed, on call Navy warship, subject to being ordered to sea at any time, in an emergency, with adequate crew. Liberty personnel was limited. This meant our ship was at anchor out in the bay, it also meant we had to return to fleet landing by midnight to catch the last Liberty boat to our ship. This was fine because I had to leave the hospital about ten o'clock anyway. During this period there were times when I was absolutely not permitted to leave my ship. By now I had been in the Navy long enough to learn to do a lot of things I was not supposed to do. If I had been caught, in this case leaving my duty post, I could have spent a lot of time in the brig. My love for Katherine was far stronger even than loyalty to my country and if necessary, I would die for my country. I found a way to see her every night. Foolish? Yes, but that's just the way it was. In hindsight, I may have done things differently, but perhaps not.

The same day Katherine was discharged from the hospital, my ship was taken off "on duty call" (this may not be the correct terminology) and could now tie up to the pier. This meant we could come and go without worrying about being on time for a Liberty boat. Later, as she regained her strength we had our first argument. She had been in the hospital and house for so long she just wanted to get out and ask me to take her for a trolley ride. Everything outside was covered with snow and thick ice. The trolley stop was blocks away. I told her it was too cold and too bad for her going out the first time. My real reason, I knew the shore patrol (S.P.) regularly rode those trolleys, checking sailors Liberty cards to be away from their base or ships and I did not have a legitimate card. For some reason I didn't tell her, I don't remember why, but for the first time I saw her express her displeasure at not getting something she wanted. Her next ten words provoked a little of the Irish in me. She said, "If you won't take me I'll find someone who will." I know it surprised her when I put on my coat, opened the door and walked out.

There was a bright full moon overhead and the snow and ice was crisp. I was walking down the street when I heard a pleading little voice, "Wally, please don't leave." I turned around and saw a lightly dressed little person standing on ice in the middle of the yard, again saying, "Please don't leave." My heart melted, I walked back, took her in my arms and for the first time, saying it like she really meant it, "I love you Wally, I don't want you to go." Those were the words I had wanted to hear since the first night I walked home with her. Words cannot describe the feeling we shared at that moment. Both our eyes were glistening with tears. I said to her, "Darling, I have loved you since the first moment I saw you in the store and my love has deepened more and more every time I think of you." We held each other tightly as we walked back into the house. We embraced for a long while, not saying a word. Our love said all that needed to be said. Our feelings were so intense, I really believe God Himself was right there again, His arms happily around both of us. He has certainly blessed our marriage. Finally, it was really time for me to go. I had to walk a pretty good ways before getting a ride to the fleet landing and my ship. The trolleys had stopped running for the night. I don't remember the cold one bit. I was again up on cloud nine and my love really did keep me warm.

During the time she was staying with Jimmy and Margaret, to help out, I took gallon cans of food to the house, green beans, peaches, peanut butter, jelly, etc. Don't ask me where it came from or how I got it off the ship, part of the mailman's job is to carry large bags of packages and mail to the post office. They were still eating peanut butter years after that.

* * * * *

Katherine was getting her strength back and wanted to go home. Hortense, the lady from Roanoke who worked at the store, the only one who told me a lot about Katherine when I first met her, wanted to do something for her. She and her husband offered to take Katherine to her home in North Carolina. This would be a one day trip. They asked me to go with them. This was my first time going to her home and meeting some of her family. I was made to feel right at home. Now, I was beginning to understand why, to me, she was really different from any girl I had ever known. I felt, at the time, this was to be a very, very special day for Katherine and me. The time was early December, 1947, a very crisp, clear, cold day. The past five years I had been totally involved in war and post war Navy, always living and working with hundreds of other men. Katherine wanted to show me more of the farm and gather some mistletoe for Christmas. We were deep in the woods and swamps of Eastern North Carolina. We walked through the chicken yard, looked into barns, petted the mule, and saw inside my first tobacco barn. Surrounded by tall forest trees, we strolled, holding hands, further into the grass covered fields where the cows grazed. This was something neither of us had been able to do for a long time, take the time to really enjoy the beauty of God's earth. As we walked in the pasture, we stopped under a small apple tree, our arms around each other, and our lips together. We each professed our deep love for the other and for the first time we talked about marriage. Too soon, the day was over.

Katherine and I had been together part of every day or night for three weeks. My heart was heavy, knowing I would not see her until the end of December. Now, my life was going to take a very dramatic, bittersweet change of course. Only a few months before, I was looking forward to staying in the Navy and enjoying an all expense paid trip around the world. I wasn't even thinking about the future. Now, I was walking away and saying goodbye to my shipmates and the ships I was so very proud of and had been my home for over two years. My magic carpet, taking me to places in the world I never knew existed, from breath taking beautiful islands in the South Seas, to frozen cold barren lands in the Arctic Ocean. They too had a magical beauty we enjoyed. We sailed the mysterious Bermuda Triangle many times and Cape Hatteras, the world's graveyard of ships, where the warm trade winds from the south meet the cold winds from the north. The ocean bottom sands constantly shifting. The Schrill Bos'n whistle on the intercom, "Now hear this, prepare the ship for heavy weather." There were tough times, but overall I really enjoyed and learned from my experiences as a crewman aboard two of the Navy's most respected type of fighting warships. I know it made me a better man. Yes, it was an emotional, sad and very private moment for me when I turned for a last look at both of my ships. They were a very important part of my life, knowing I would probably never see either of them again. With my sea bag on my shoulder, I saluted each, turned and walked into my new life, with the woman I love, forever. Absolutely no regrets.

Our love had a beginning, but there will never be an ending. One of our children, now grown up, said, "Dad, yours and mom's was a marriage made in heaven." What a wonderful feeling knowing that any one of our children could have said those words. We have no problem letting our children know and see that we respect and love each other.

* * * * *

I was assigned to quarters on the Norfolk Naval Base near the barracks I was in while waiting to go to my first ship at Portland, Maine. Now, I was waiting to receive my honorable discharge papers from the Navy. I received them in time to be home for Christmas for the first time in four years. Also, the beginning of our five month, mostly long distance courtship, more than a hundred love letters were written by each of us. We each saved those letters and read them fifty-five years later. I enjoyed being with my family but my thoughts and my heart were with a certain young lady, recuperating at her home, on a tobacco farm in Eastern North Carolina and that is where I was heading, on a trailways bus, December 26, 1947. Exactly four years to the day when I left home for the Navy.

Katherine and a brother met me at the station in Washington, North Carolina. We drove to the farm about five miles beyond Pinetown. I put that week, in my entire life, at the top of my list. It was one of the most restful, peaceful, enjoyable weeks of my life, and I had my darling Katherine back in my arms. For the first time in more than six years, I could completely relax. I did not have to report to anyone, be anywhere at any time to do anything I did or did not want to do. I did not have to wear a uniform or observe protocol and regulations. I also did not have a job and I didn't care. The only thing I did have to do, after the rooster crowed, was hope I could make it in time to the "two holer" out by the chicken yard. If that was occupied the next choice was behind the barn or into the woods. I no longer had to share a bathroom with a hundred other guys. The whole outdoors was all mine, every tree. When I learned what the pecan or thunder mug in my room was for, I could not figure a way to hide it or carry it downstairs without everybody seeing me. When I got up earlier I noticed everyone else had to do the same thing. By the third morning I was even brave enough to pump fresh water into mine, rinse it out and let it dry.

The first morning I thought I was in heaven when I woke up and saw two beautiful, sparkling eyes looking down at me and heard a nice soft voice saying, "Wake up, breakfast will soon be ready," and receiving a sweet little kiss before she disappeared out the door. It was tough getting out of a nice warm bed in that cold room. I rushed downstairs and into the real "country kitchen" to a real "country breakfast". The smell of fresh hot coffee, bacon frying, freshly made biscuits baking in a wood fired oven; there is nothing to compare it with. My first meal, prepared by the precious gift God was offering to me, to have, to hold, to love, to cherish, to blend our lives together, forever.

The next morning I was first to get up and went into her room. She promptly ran me out before momma found me in her bedroom. "What a revoltin situation" that was, and I didn't even get a kiss. If I had not drank too much water the night before, every morning after that, I slept until she came into my room.

Mother Jackson had been widowed four years. She was a soft spoken, gentle woman. Having raised six sons and two daughters, she knew very well how to clip the feathers of any young rooster, meaning me, that came into the flock. I loved and had great admiration and respect for her.

This was to be the most meaningful period of our seven month courtship. We were actually living on a day to day basis in the same house, about sixteen hours each day for eight days, giving us enough time in everyday living to experience the needs, the habits, the many moods, temperaments, feelings, and nature of each other. I also learned, after we were married, that the Lord threw in a couple of the very delicate days all young women endure each month. I got to see her without makeup, without every golden strand of hair in place, with a bandanna around her head while washing, hanging up wet clothes, ironing, all the old fashioned no electricity, build a fire under the wash pot out in the yard, scrub board, grandma's lye soap, sweating way. We even had fun when I helped shampoo her hair out on the screened in back porch using water from a hand pump and heated on the wood fire kitchen stove. A few months later in one of her letters, she wrote about telling her roommate at the Y.W.C.A. about this and laughing. She said I had seen her at her ugliest and she could not see what I saw in her, but she sure was glad I did see something.

The family came together each night in the living room, a nice hot fire in the wood stove. Television had not yet invaded and destroyed the very fabric and closeness that bonds families and friends together. The battery powered radio was used by farmers for weather and news. You do not miss something you never had. Neighbors sometimes dropped in for a nice visit, no telephones. We actually enjoyed talking for hours, playing games, or reading, and as the fire died down, each of us drifted off to crawl into bed, under a pile of blankets with our feet pulled up close. A glass of water on the table beside the bed would turn to ice overnight. I don't remember and I guess it was too early in our courting for me to dream of her being right there beside me and keeping each other warm, but I am sure at some time, I must have thought about Katherine being in one bed freezing and me in another in the next room.

I spent several hours each day just walking as deep into the woods as time would allow. The weather was cold but after all those years being surrounded by hundreds of men, it was pure pleasure to be where I could not see or hear another human being. All alone, enjoying God's creatures and creation. The sounds, the smell, the taste of clean, fresh, crisp air, the feel of nature enfolding me just felt good. I met more of Katherine's family and with each one I became more anxious and proud that someday soon I may become a member of this fine family. Her younger sister and I became good buddies. We chopped and carried a lot of fire wood together. She made really good pies but was a lousy checkers player. I let her win a few times just to make her feel good. Now, if you ask her about that she will tell you it was the other way around, but you know I would never tell a fib.

As always, when I was with Katherine, the time passed far too quickly, just as it is doing even today, nearly sixty years later. We celebrated our first New Years together, 1947-48, in her living room. We were alone on the couch. We kissed the old year out and the new year in as we sat with our arms around each other. I whispered softly, in my most romantic tone, into her ear, "I love you darling with all my heart, do you love me?" She looked at me with those big, beautiful, sparkling eyes, and said ---very emphatically --- "NO!!!" My mouth dropped open, my eyes must have bulged, "Boy what a revoltin development this is." Then she grabbed me, kissed me over and over and said, "Yes, yes, yes, yes." It was chilly in that room but I felt sweat on my brow. I learned something else about her; she had a sadistic sense of humor, (not really). I knew she didn't mean it, but I just could not get it out of my mind. The very first word she said to me in 1948, when I wanted her to say she loved me, was "NO," maybe I'm a little superstitious. Yes, it did bother me for a while but we laugh about it now.

The time for recuperating from her operation was drawing to a close. The room rent at the "Y" was due, doctor and hospital bills had to be paid. Time to go back to work. To show you the difference between a dollar bill in 1947 and the same dollar at whatever time you read this, the following is copied from the original hospital stay in 1947. I found them in an old suitcase with our love letters more than fifty-seven years later, also her 1947 W-2 tax withholding form.

* * * * *

NAME JACKSON MIS CATHERENE
ADDRESS 240 W FREEMASON ST
MEMO 9983

#	Date	Explanation	Amt. Charged	Amt. Credited	Bal. Due
1					
2					
3					
4					
5	NOV24 47	LABRY	10.00		
6	NOV24 47	WARD	6.00		16.00
7	NOV25 47	WARD	6.00		
8	NOV25 47	DRUGS	3.60		25.60
9	NOV26 47	WARD	6.00		
10	NOV26 47	DRUGS	3.50		
11	NOV26 47	OP-RM	15.00		
12	NOV26 47	ANAES	15.00		
13	NOV26 47	DRUGS	0.60		65.70
14	NOV28 47	WARD	6.00		
15	NOV28 47	DRUGS	6.00		
16	NOV28 47			6.00	
17	NOV28 47	WARD	6.00		77.70
18	NOV28 47	DRUGS	5.50		
19	NOV28 47	DRUGS	0.70		83.90
20	NOV29 47	WARD	6.00		89.90
21	NOV30 47	WARD	6.00		95.90
22	NOV30 47	COM. PAID		95.90	0.00
23					
24					

STATEMENT
ALL ACCOUNTS ARE DUE AND PAYABLE WEEKLY IN ADVANCE
DE PAUL HOSPITAL
NORFOLK 5, VA.

November 24, 1947 – Emergency, appendicitis – rushed to hospital: <u>Seven</u> days – food – drugs – anesthesia – operating room – laboratory →**$95.90** Doctors Bill →**$95.00**

I used to think she married me for my money but then I remembered I was only making $35.00 a week for two of us, so it must have been my "good looks", charm, debonair, witty, there's a few more but I can't think of them right now. How about worldly – enchanting and romantic, lover – to be continued sweet -thoughtful - -

[Withholding Statement – 1947, Form W-2, Employee's Copy. Katherine Jackson, YWCA, Norfolk, Virginia. Total Wages Paid in 1947: 1029.00; Federal Income Tax Withheld: 103.1. United Cigar-Whelan Stores Corporation, 215 Fourth Ave. New York 3, N.Y.]

We have all used or heard someone make the statement, "The Lord works in strange ways." Well, this certainly proves that old "saying" to be true. When I began these writings putting dates and times together, Katherine and I were trying to remember the months she arrived in Norfolk and the month my ship sailed into Hampton Roads about a year later. Fifty-seven years later, under a pile of other stuff, we discovered an old suitcase filled with the hundreds of love letters we had written to each other. We also found an old envelope containing her first "withholding statement, income tax form," giving us the exact date she started working, she arrived two days before that in 1946.

The W-2 withholding form you see here is for the <u>entire year</u> of 1947: $1029.00 - - - about $2.80 per work day, all expenses including room rent were paid from this and she even bought clothing.

* * * * *

Katherine's older brother, next to her, worked in Portsmouth, Virginia, a short ferry ride from Norfolk. We were riding with him the three hour drive back to Norfolk. He had a date that night with the girl he would later marry. Katherine and I were in the back seat and by the time he took her home and we arrived in Norfolk we had spent our first night together in the back seat of her brother's car. We had a very tired day together. First thing, taking her suitcase to her room at the Y.W.C.A., I had to wait in the parlor. Then we walked the six blocks to the drug store to get her work schedule. We enjoyed some hours at our favorite park, strolling by the lake, holding hands, realizing our love for each other was soon to be put to the ultimate test. She would be going back to her job and living her life as a single girl, by herself, in a city surrounded by Army, Marine, and Navy bases and ships. Temptation beyond belief for an attractive, blonde, young, single girl. We had met only three months ago, and most of that time I was on my ship at sea. Could our love possibly survive such a trial?

The time span for our realizing we each had fallen deeply in love with the other was only about six weeks. For me it started the moment I first saw her. For Katherine, her feelings for me beyond the friendship stage began to blossom during my nightly visits while she was in the hospital and climaxed the night we had a little disagreement while she was regaining her strength at her friend's home. When I put on my coat and walked out, she realized then, she just could not let me walk out of her life. During December, in several of her letters, she wrote how she no longer had any doubt about her love for me. She came home to regain her strength after her operation and Mother Jackson would not allow her to do any work. She spent her day in the warm living room making doilies for her sister and writing a letter to me each day while watching for the mailman to bring the letters I was writing. Several times she did not receive my letters for several days and became very upset with me but then received three or four all at one time. Then came the week we spent together at her home. Could the feelings we had, the promises and plans we made in such a short time sustain us during at least four months we would mostly be apart, except for short visits?

      Our week together was soon to end. We were walking toward the train station onto the passenger platform where the train was waiting and as always, holding hands. My heart was breaking as I took her into my arms, we kissed, let go our hands and I stepped onto the train. I found a seat where we could see each other through the window. As the train moved away, just before she disappeared from my view, I saw her take a handkerchief from her pocket and wipe tears from her eyes. She looked so small and lonely, standing by herself on the walkway. As the train picked up speed there are no words to describe my feelings at that moment. Now, I had a little taste of what the married guys with children went through, being away from their families for possibly years. Some returned to children who did not remember their father, others who had never even seen him. Too many never returned.

Katherine walked back to her room at the Y.W.C.A. and wrote me a sweet little letter while I was still on the train. When I began these writings, things I had long forgotten or just had not thought of for all those years, began to unfold, like pages of a book, one thought or series of thoughts led to another. Like thousands of others, we put away our war toys and let memories of war fade into the past and began putting our lives together and building for the future. I don't remember even talking about the war or the Navy. With tens of thousands of us returning home, except for the first greetings of family and friends, I don't remember any parades or welcome home celebrations. We were not treated, expect or feel like heroes or someone special until years later when the twin towers went down. Suddenly people were shaking my hand and thanking me for what we did sixty years ago. We didn't realize we were making and were a very important part of American history. Someone even wrote a book calling us "The Greatest Generation".

I just got on a train in Norfolk, came home to start my life out of the Navy and faced a reality that had not occurred to me. I was so young before going into the Navy. I had worked at only one real job, building war ships, not a very marketable job skill just after a war. The post office employment was filled. In other words, I had no marketable skills. Income producing jobs were being snapped up even before they were available and long lines waiting for each one. I guess you could call me "a man on a mission". In spite of the mountainous obstacles, I knew I could not ask Katherine's hand in marriage until I could support a wife. My love for Katherine drove my every thought and decision. She was the focus of every goal I set.

* * * * *

Plastic was for most people unheard of at that time, I had worked with something called plastic at an airbase. I heard about a man coming to town who was introducing plastic to businesses in the south and needed help. I decided to give it a try. The company manufactured table covers, aprons, chair seats, automobile seat covers etc. They advertised in restaurants, cars, clubs, and magazines. We received the orders and inquiries, called on the accounts and received commissions on sales and future orders. This was a learning process important to me for two reasons. It was good money at the time and I learned I was a pretty good salesman. This experience followed me the rest of my life. With only a ninth grade education I would never have made it up the corporate ladder.

With my discharge pay from the Navy, I had bought a diamond engagement ring before leaving my home town and was going to propose marriage to Katherine when I returned to Norfolk. I was afraid it would be stolen or lost during my travel. I mailed it to her in January 1948. She was excited but let me know she was disappointed I was not there to put it on her finger. We wrote almost daily letters to each other but I sensed my traveling was beginning to take its toll.

Katherine's letters were sent to general delivery in each city I was in and sometimes I would receive four or five letters at one time, several were returned to her. Because of my sales, my boss gave me a promotion. The second Saturday in February I had written Katherine's letter, I did not have a three cent stamp to mail it and the post office was closed. I looked at that letter and decided what I was gaining was not worth what I may be losing. I decided I was going to deliver that letter in person. My roommate was out to a dance, I wrote a note to tell the boss I had to return home right away. I called the Greyhound bus station. The bus to Norfolk would leave at four o'clock in the morning, at 2:00 AM I started walking the two miles to the station. Due to bus changes and layovers I did not arrive in Norfolk until Monday afternoon.

    Telephones were few and far between but I did call the store from a bus station. Katherine was busy with a customer, I was told the time she would be off work but forgot to ask him to tell her I was on my way. I was so anxious and nervous about seeing her, but I had been traveling for two days and needed a shower and shave. I checked in for a bunk at the Navy "Y" and cleaned up. I did not want to be in the store when we would first see each other so I waited across the street. She came out the door with two other girls. When I first saw her come out the door, I got the same feeling as when she appeared in my vision that Sunday morning my shipmate and I walked into the store for breakfast. She took my breath and my heart. She looked my way while crossing the street but did not recognize me because she was used to seeing me in my Navy blues. She did a double take when she realized it was me and came running into my arms. We had three wonderful days, walking, talking, renewing our love, and making plans. The third night we double dated with another couple, going to a nice club with a small dance band. This would later create a problem for us.

* * * * *

The following day, my train was scheduled to leave after Katherine would be going to work. I was glad it worked out that way because I just did not want again to see her standing all alone on that train station platform and disappear as the train pulled out. She was really happy I would be going back home and not traveling anymore. I was again heading back home to start all over again. This time the Lord was with me. I was at the right place at the right time to quickly find a job with a "Veterans Administration Regional Office" in downtown Roanoke. I was hired as a "file clerk". The records of tens of thousands of veterans and military personnel were maintained and stored here. Computers were many years into the future. Each day hundreds of medical records, forms, letters, and general information had to be hand pulled or filed into numbered files in hundreds of file cabinets lined around an entire floor in the building. The cabinets were lined facing the wall. Now for the good part, on the other side of the cabinets were dozens of desks, at each desk was a young female typist, busy all day typing correspondence, medical records, or forms. Stop getting ahead of me!! But you guessed it, put young people close and they will find each other using different techniques. The guys will check out a new girl and the girls will check out a new guy coming in.

The guys could not go around the file cabinets and bother the girls but if there was one he was interested in there is an age old technique called eye contact. He would "accidently", on purpose, let her catch him watching her. If she was interested in him she would pretend to be reading and coyly let him catch her looking his way. This could go on for several days. Their eyes would meet and if she gave him a little under the brow smile he would find a way to talk with her. The girls would use a more direct approach. If there was a guy she was interested in, she would simply mention it to another girl who would write a little note and pass it on to the guy, telling him, "Suzie likes you, give her a call at this number." Yes, I did receive a few notes, I wrote a note back. "Thank you for the nice compliment, I am engaged and totally committed to another wonderful girl, we will marry in the near future." I guess the word got around because there were no other notes to me. Hey, I just had a revoltin thought when I wrote that last sentence, maybe there weren't going to be any more notes to me. Oh well, I can dream can't I?

* * * * *

Before I was any more than a friend to Katherine, we attended a party in a private home. A girl from Roanoke was at the party and Katherine later said she was trying to take me away from her. This girl had a way of unexpectedly showing up. After I came back to Roanoke, she walked into the drug store where Katherine was working and started asking questions about me, this made Katherine a bit angry and I believe when she sensed competition, it made her even more determined I might be worth keeping. Hubba Hubba, Now things were really going my way. The girl returned to Roanoke and called my home several times. I answered the third time and she told me my mom would not let her talk to me. I found out I had calls from other girls and mom would not tell me unless the call was from Norfolk. I can't decide if mom was on my side or not. Anyway, I can honestly say, each time I held Katherine in my arms and kissed her goodbye, no other girl was in my arms, no girls' lips touched mine until I returned to my Katherine.

* * * * *

Shopping centers were unheard of until the mid 1950's, before that just about all business of every type was conducted in what everyone called the downtown area. A store like Katherine worked in, lunch counter, pharmacy, tobacco, beauty supplies, etc had many, everyday customers. One of those customers was an older bachelor who owned his own deluxe taxi cab. He was in the store just about every day. His name was Max. I called him, "Old Max". We learned to hate each other. "Old Max" took a liking to Katherine long before I met her. When she started working at the store, Old Max was the first to take her to a really nice seafood restaurant. She still talks about having the first scallops she had ever tasted, taken fresh from local waters, and how much she liked and enjoyed scallops.

"Old Max" seemed to have plenty of money. When she had a long weekend off, he would offer to give her a ride to her home in Carolina, which at times she accepted. He would take her straight to her home. Then, go to a motel in town and return to take her back to Norfolk. This continued for most of the time before I came into the picture. Katherine considered him as just a real nice friend, but to Max it was a lot more. He had to realize he was 15-20 years older than she and he was competing with younger men. But, I believe he was hoping that over time she would realize he was there for her and it would develop into more than just a friendship. When I began to come into her life and he could see that I was more than just another sailor who would disappear as soon as his ship was assigned to another distant port, he began showing signs of his displeasure and jealously. Katherine's mother warned her to leave him alone, she was concerned. She had known of others like this where the older man had decided, if he could not have the girl, no one would have her.

I hated Old Max at that time, but it is really strange how time can make you see even unpleasant things, in an entirely different perspective. Over the years I have come to understand and see his side of this part of our lives. I now understand and believe that Max saw the same qualities in Katherine that I saw. In his time going to her home and me in my time going to her home, we saw the environment she was raised in, a strong, loving, Christian family, each having respect and a great love for the other. This shone through brightly in the fine young lady, woman, wife, and mother she turned out to be. I absolutely believe the Lord gave me the ability to see her beyond the influences of a seaport town. I thought she was the prettiest girl I had ever seen, so her beauty was the first to get my attention. She was aloof to her male customers just enough not to appear flirty, just as she was to me the first time she waited on me. A friendly, young sales clerk trying to give her employer's customers good service.

* * * * *

Now all of this does not mean there were no incidents. Katherine had been promoted to the "over the counter drug department." Keep in mind there was a time until the last few years that certain items designed and made strictly for male use, were not blatantly displayed on store shelves. When a member of the male gender had need for them, he would quietly ask a male pharmacist, who would go to a special drawer back in the pharmacy, hold them unseen in his hand, and place them in the hand of the customer. Things were beginning to change. A male customer came to Katherine and asked her for a package of condoms. She had to go to the druggist and ask him, "What is a condom?" He smiled and told her he would take care of it. He also asked one of the older married ladies to explain to her about condoms. She told me about this after we were married. She was now twenty-three years old, I thought this was so cute and funny, in a nice way. It also told me something every young man about to be married, would be extremely happy to learn about the girl who would someday be his wife.

* * * * *

Our marriage has been wonderful and just about as perfect as a marriage could possibly be. Our long distance courtship almost just the opposite, not because of what either of us did, but what others perceived was going on and made sure we were told.

Our letter writing almost every night and phone calls was the bond that held our love together and we survived all of the pitfalls of being apart. The one time I was really angry with Katherine, and yes, jealous, was when one of her girlfriend's boyfriend that she and I had double dated with for an evening of dancing and fun, let it be known that he really liked Katherine and wanted to date her. We were engaged at that time and I was back in Roanoke. She told him she was not dating. He persisted, he called her, came to the drug store where she worked and begged her to let him come back and talk with her. She finally gave in, knowing very well he did not want to talk to her about the weather, sports, or the price of eggs in China. All she had to do was raise her left hand, show him her ring and tell him there was nothing he had to say that she needed to hear. Most guys would respect a girl wearing an engagement ring if they could see that she was really trying to be true to her fiancé. Many of them were young guys, engaged to a girl back home. This dude was a creep and thought he was God's gift to women, not an honorable man. He wanted her to leave me and go with him. She told me she sent him on his way.

  I had dated several girls in Norfolk before I met Katherine and we started dating regular. They happen to be friends who worked with her at the store. But I did not meet them at the store. The CPO Club was a large and popular place, probably fifty or more tables that would seat 6-8 people. I was there maybe three times before I met Katherine and each time I seemed to be directed to one section and one table, of course girls would usually sit together at other places in the room. I had no special interest in any one girl at that table and I had not met Katherine. The odds were high against me going to that particular table the night I did meet her. This turned out to be a good thing because one of those girls introduced us and was the same girl who asked me to walk with Katherine to the Y.W.C.A. the night we met at the CPO Club dance. We found out later she was angry with Katherine for taking me away from her. This caused some problems later.

I was at my home in Roanoke when I received a call from a girl in Norfolk asking me if I knew that Katherine was dating the tall guy? The one who tried to get her to leave me, that kept coming in the store. When I talked with Katherine about this she promised that she had not dated him or anyone else. I chose to believe my Katherine.

* * * * *

We also had another problem that could have created some serious situations. Katherine often worked the evening shift at the store and did not get off until eleven o'clock at night. From the store to the Y.W.C.A. was about six blocks. No city, especially downtown Norfolk, then or now is safe for an attractive young woman to be walking by herself at that time of night. She did this many times and had to endure the insults from men on the street. I realized this could be a very dangerous time and she would not always have another girl to walk with. The newspaper would tell of young girls' bodies being found in backwashes in the area and the mobsters who were known to force young women into prostitution. This was a time when most people knew little or nothing about the deadly effects of drugs or how their bodies could become addicted to drugs. But just as today the human slime made it their business to know how to force decent, pretty young girls into prostitution by injecting addictive drugs into their bodies and forcing them to sell their bodies for the money to buy drugs for their addiction.

While I was in the Navy I was in sickbay for a badly sprained ankle and shared a room for a week with a guy who was a former member of an organized crime gang in California. He said no one just quits, you either die or try to get lost. If they had not been convicted of a felony, they often joined the military and try to get far away from those who know them as members. They were expected to do anything and everything to bring money into the organization. He knew he was marked and could not lead a normal life until years had passed. Katherine was brought up in the closed society of a farm girl. She was taught to trust people. She did not fully realize the possible danger she was in. She worked in a public position, talking with strangers all day. When she worked until eleven at night, and had to walk by herself, she took one of only two ways to walk to the Y.W.C.A. Just as with me, her "Guardian Angel" had to have been with her many times. She was the perfect choice and an easy target for those who could have done her harm. They could know exactly when she would leave the store and the time when she would be walking through the more secluded, darkened spots on her way to the "Y". It would have taken only seconds for her to disappear into a van or car. I knew this from talking with those who may have done these very things. I expressed my concerns but she had made this walk many times before we met and because nothing had happened that she could not handle she felt reasonably safe.

A known mob member had already asked her for a date but her co-workers told her to stay far away from him. I did not want to overly frighten her but I did ask her to try to always have someone she knew to walk with her. I knew very well it would not always be another girl. I also knew that guys who walked with her would be expecting more than just holding hands and some were very aggressive. Walking her home was how I got to know her. Since she grew up in an area where people trusted and helped each other, she was not prepared for those who would take advantage of her trusting innocence and I could not be there for her. I also was aware that she knew right from wrong and could be stubborn when the need was there.

By this time I loved Katherine deeply, so much that I would rather lose her to another man than have something very bad happen to her. I have learned her exterior, gentle shyness betrays a strong inner strength. Being raised as a farm girl with six brothers and a strict father helped her to handle situations that come to many young women.

* * * * *

The following is a very sensitive area for both Katherine and me. I ask that if you do not have the time to read this part in its entirety, then please wait until you do have the time. We feel we should share it with you just on the possibility it may be of help to other young couples who are going through a similar difficult part of their long distance courting days. At some point, your faith, your trust in one or the other or each of you will be put to the ultimate test.

We knew we would not be together for possibly a month or more at times. We talked about how to avoid the gossip that could come up. We also knew there may be misunderstandings between us and possibly caused by others. We agreed if we went to a dance or party we would not have a date and would tell the other about it before going, just in case someone did call.

About six weeks before our wedding day, on a Sunday evening, my family was out, I was at home alone. I received a phone call from one of Katherine's friends at the Y.W.C.A. with the most devastating news, other than her death, a young man could possibly receive at this point of our engagement and plans for our future. The first thing she asked, "Are you and Katherine still engaged and planning to be married?" I said, "Yes, as far as I knew we are." She started to cry and said, "Wally, I have to tell you something that is going to break your heart," how right she was. "Last night I was with the boy I am engaged to, at The "Palms". I know you have been there, one of the nicest private dance clubs in Norfolk, where married or engaged couples can go. Men without escorts are not admitted. It was crowded and we were on the dance floor when I saw the back of a girl with long blonde hair, as we moved closer I saw it was Katherine. She was dancing with a tall sailor; it was obvious she had a date. Later as the crowd thinned out, I could see them and the others at her table leaving the club. We were sitting at a table where I could see out a window. It was very cold out and the girls were under the sailors' coats. I could see only Katherine's hair. As you know, there is a motel just down the street from the club. Wally, I watched them go into that motel. My date and I had to rush to make it back to the "Y" before they locked the door at one o'clock. My room is just across the hall from hers. It is late Sunday afternoon, she still has not returned to the 'Y'."

If what I had been told by this friend of hers and mine was true, she was still with him at that very moment. She had told me nothing about a dance. By this time we had each written about one hundred letters to the other. We were both often asked by friends how we could write so many letters. They were unable to understand our commitment and actually being true to each other. Letters almost every day and we stuck to it for five and a half months. All of our dreams, our plans, our entire life. If I had not met Katherine, I would at that time still be in the Navy for at least four more years. Just signing the papers would have given me a nice extra reenlistment bonus. When I was called to report to the executive officers quarters to sign the papers, he could not believe it when I told him I was going to take my walking papers (discharge). He tried his best to talk me into reenlisting. I was the ships only rated mailman and the only one on board that was qualified and had a Navy chauffeur's license. But now I had found the girl that I loved and I could not ask her to wait a year or more for me. I never dreamed a broken heart could hurt this badly. If this were true, it would be the end for Katherine and me. The news I had just received was more than I could handle. Suddenly my entire world had come crashing down, my imagination was going wild. This was a good friend of hers. We had double dated with her and her fiancé. She was in the room when Katherine received her engagement ring. If it had been anyone but her that called I don't know that I would have believed them. She had no reason to call and tell me something like this if she did not believe it to be true.

* * * * *

The next two days are a complete blur in my memory. I lost about three pounds which I could not afford to lose. I also lost three days at my new job, but I just did not care. My mom thought I was nervous about the wedding. She kept bringing me food, which I could not eat, and medicine. I just couldn't tell her what had happened. Wednesday I went to the Navy recruiting station and picked up papers to reenlist in the Navy. While filling them in I remembered there was only one person who may know about this and would tell me the truth. This was my good friend Jimmy who welcomed Katherine into his home after her surgery. I called and Jimmy answered the phone. I told him about the phone call I had received, but not about the motel. I asked if Katherine was with his sister, did she have a date, and did she spend the night with her at his house? He could tell I was extremely upset. He said, "Yes, Wally, I do know something about Saturday night, but I don't know anything about Katherine having a date. I spent most of that night putting in a new water heater. I heard the car drive up about 1:30 or 2:00. Sis stayed out in the car shelter saying goodnight to her boyfriend and Katherine came right in and went to their room. Evidently, she did not have a date." The "Palms

Club" closed at one o'clock. I knew the drive to Jimmy's house was about thirty minutes. He said, "They spent most of Sunday doing girl things and later I took her back to the "Y"." I said, "Thanks Jimmy, someday I may be able to tell you what this call has done for me, but right now I just can't do it."

* * * * *

The letter she wrote on Monday was delivered Thursday. I called her Wednesday night, she told me her friends had asked her last Wednesday to go to a dance with them Saturday night. She told them she had too much work to do on her day off. Saturday she slept late, cleaned her room, washed and ironed clothes, and washed and set her hair. When her friends called again and asked her to go with them and their dates, she decided she needed a break and would go. She had just enough time to get ready before they came by. This explained everything except the motel, I had to know. Finally, I told her I had received a call from someone who told me she watched you going into a motel with sailors. I could hear her gasp, finally she said, the only thing I can tell you about that, it was a little late when we arrived at the club, the parking lot was full so the car was parked on the far side of the motel and we walked back to the club. After the dance, when we walked back to the car we had to pass right by the entrance to the motel, we certainly did not go inside and we drove straight to Jimmy's house. This explained everything. The girl who called me, in the crowded dimly lit club, could not see only two sailors and three girls at their table. Her view through the window, when they walked two buildings away from the club at night and turned the corner of the building just past the motel entrance, it may have looked like they did go in the door. She did not know Katherine had a girlfriend to spend the night with. I knew then that my Katherine had done nothing I would not approve of.

I did, late that Sunday, receive another call from a shipmate who was at the same club and thought I should know she was dating other guys. This only confirmed what I had already been told. The trauma of all this did affect me for a long time. At this point my entire future was planned around her. My love for her was so deep there are no words that can properly describe how much I truly loved this wonderful woman. I had never told her the complete story until more than fifty years later when I decided to do these writings. We both cried until we realized the happiness we have shared was worth whatever it took for us to be together. Before they knew I was very serious about her, I had been told other things by other guys about Katherine. I didn't know if they were true or not, I just knew I did not find her to be that way and guys like to brag about their conquests, especially with a girl as pretty as she. I suppose most girls are victims of this to some degree. I do know this, on our wedding night, I found that my faith and trust in my darling Katherine was more than justified. She presented herself to me and gave to me the most precious gift of love that a bride can possibly give to the man she has chosen to be her lifelong companion and the father of her children. She says she was a dummy and naïve about a lot of things. I say she was among the smartest women on earth because of who she is and how she had conducted herself in spite of being single and living almost alone in a major seaport city. She had no one to account to or advise her or even care what she did or did not do. She had to have faced a lot of temptations. She is honored by her children who show their love and admiration for their mother and a husband who truly loves, admires and adores her after more than sixty years of happiness (2008). There are four verses in the Bible that were written for my Katherine: Proverbs 31:10, 11, 12, and especially 28. Her children rise up and call her blessed; her husband also, and he praises her.

* * * * *

When Katherine and I knew we were ready for marriage, she knew no one in my hometown and she had many friends in Norfolk. She decided that was where the wedding would be, but it wasn't, with the help of a friend, she found the minister she liked in Portsmouth, Virginia, just a fifteen minute ferry ride across the river from Norfolk. Katherine and her best girlfriend, who was also her bridesmaid, had to make all of the elaborate arrangements, which was knowing the time to show up at the minister's home with a few friends and family members. No big bands, banquets, photographers, truck loads of gifts, new car outside, or off to the South Seas islands. Just a friend with a brownie camera, my big brother and "Best Man loaned me his car to drive away, decorated, from the minister's home to a small restaurant in town. I can't remember if I ever gave him the twenty-five dollars to pay the minister.

    Katherine and I had all that we needed to start our life together, our Lord's blessing and our deep love for each other. Our marriage certificate says, "So then they are no more twain but one flesh," and so with God's help, it has come to pass. There are five boys in my family, each of us have celebrated our Golden Wedding Anniversary, fifty years plus. So the Hillman boys have a good record for finding beautiful ladies who made good wives. Of course, good looks and humility run in the Hillman family.

During the day just before the wedding, mom kept telling me the weight I had lost seemed to be all in my face. I think she was worried that Katherine would change her mind when she saw me. When I look closely at the few wedding pictures we have, I can see why she would think that.

* * * * *

Saturday, the day before the wedding, my brother Al, his wife and I arrived in Norfolk late afternoon. We went directly to Jimmy and Margaret's home, the friends Katherine stayed with after her surgery. They were to spend the night there. I was to stay at the "Navy Y" and Katherine was to bunk in with the friend who first brought her to Norfolk. Part of this worked out. Al loaned me his car to go see my bride to be, we were together a few hours, when we went to her friend's apartment in a private home, we could not get in. We threw pebbles at windows in her upstairs apartment, no response. She no longer had a room at the Y.W.C.A., she could not stay at the "Navy Y", only one other place, back to Jimmy's. They were all in bed. It's hard to believe but there was once a time when people didn't bother to lock their doors at night. The only place we could sleep was on the couch, everyone else was in bed. She slept at one end, I slept at the other. No, there was no "Hanky Panky". I learned the hard way when I spent several days with my shipmates laughing at the red finger prints on one side of my face. All I did was what all sailors are trained to do, feel your way around in the dark. I didn't see it coming, there wasn't even a little dipper in all those stars. Boy, come morning we sure surprised everyone when they found us on the couch, they even believed our story and it was the first time my brother and his wife met Katherine, think about that one.

The wedding over, we started the three hundred mile trip back to Roanoke, arriving after dark, about 10:00 PM. After so many letters and phone calls, my mom, youngest brother, and little sister felt like they already knew Katherine. My entire family already loved her. My next to oldest brother and his wife were waiting to carry us on the last part of our journey. Our honeymoon was at Natural Bridge, Virginia. We have many times reminisced, laughed, and fondly remembered something very special just to us. The nervous young bride went into the bathroom to change into her nice new nightgown, given to her just for this special night. While an equally nervous young groom put on his nice new pajamas, bought just for this very special night and nervously waited with great anticipation for his young bride to appear.

--------- He waited --------- he waited --------- and he waited --------- he began to squirm, and waited --- and slowly the door opened. His breath taking, beautiful, young bride finally appeared --------- with tears in her eyes --------- I tenderly took her into my arms and asked if something was wrong? She laid her face on my chest and tearfully said, "I am afraid, --------- I have never been with a man." We had mentioned and dreamed of this night many times in our letters. We were so much in love.

Katherine had many "firsts" to look forward to. Her second was seeing mountains for the first time the next morning. She was so cute as she looked around in amazement. She said, "I didn't know mountains had trees on them." A lot of cowboy movies were made back then, usually where there were no trees on the western mountains. That night we watched the beautiful "Pageant of Lights", the story in Genesis, starting with the first day of the creation of earth, under the Natural Bridge. This was our first day of being together for the rest of our lives. We had three magical days of our honeymoon, getting to know each other and getting use to being, Mr. and Mrs. Wally Hillman before I had to be back on my job.

I look back over a story book life of simple living, hard work, and fantastic adventure. Finding just the right and only girl I have ever loved, to share our lives together. The success of whatever we have achieved is reflected by our three beloved children of whom we are so very proud. It has been wonderful. We will soon celebrate our sixtieth wedding anniversary in 2008. There were some rough spots along the way, as in every life. Nothing we could not handle together. We loved our way through them. We are strong in our faith. We sincerely believe that God made us for each other. Each day I thank my heavenly Father for giving me this wonderful lady, to be the mother of my children. We are in our eighties now, and as the sun slips into the evening of our lives, I look forward to walking into eternity, with my lady, forever loving and holding hands.

"I love you my darling wife."
Wally

I hope you enjoyed my
"True Adventure Stories."
If so, please tell your
Friends about my book.

                  Thank you

                  Wally